Private Equity and Healthcare: Leadership, Economics, and Trends for the Future

❖ ❖ ❖

MAX REIBOLDT, CPA

COKER

American Association for
PHYSICIAN
LEADERSHIP

Published by **American Association for Physician Leadership, Inc.**
PO Box 96503 | BMB 97493 | Washington, DC 20090-6503

Website: www.physicianleaders.org

AAPL books are available at special quantity discounts to use as premiums and sales promotions, or for use in corporate training programs. For more information, please write to Special Sales at journal@physicianleaders.org

This publication is designed to provide general information and is sold with the understanding that neither the author nor the publisher is engaged in rendering legal, accounting, ethical, or clinical advice. If legal or other expert advice is required, the services of a competent professional person should be sought.

13   8 7 6 5 4 3 2 1

Copyedited, typeset, indexed, and printed in the United States of America

PUBLISHER
Nancy Collins

PRODUCTION MANAGER
Jennifer Weiss

DESIGN & LAYOUT
Carter Publishing Studio

COPYEDITOR
Patricia George

Table of Contents

About the Authors

Private Equity in Healthcare is the combined work of Coker Group consultants who have accumulated years of experience working with healthcare concerns in financial medical management. We appreciate the opportunity to work with AAPL to offer this knowledge to its membership. Contributors include:

Max Reiboldt

Max Reiboldt, CPA, chairman of Coker, has years of invaluable experience working primarily with healthcare providers. He handles strategic, tactical, financial, and management issues that health systems, physicians, and other healthcare entities and/or investors face in today's evolving marketplace.

Max understands the nuances of the healthcare industry and their need to maintain viability in a highly competitive market. He works with organizations to provide sound solutions to everyday and long-range challenges. Clients value his open communication skills, responsiveness, and hands-on approach.

Mark Reiboldt

Mark Reiboldt is an executive vice president and director of strategy at Coker, where he specializes in financial and transaction advisory for hospitals, medical groups, and other healthcare organizations. These transactions include mergers and acquisitions, divestitures, equity purchases, physician alignment deals, and joint ventures.

John Reiboldt

John Reiboldt is Coker's chief development officer. John has many years of experience in healthcare services as an investment banker and management consultant. His consulting work encompasses mergers and acquisitions transactions, divestitures, equity purchases, physician alignment, and joint ventures.

Chad Eckhardt, Attorney, Frost Brown Todd

Chad Eckhardt leads the firm's Health Care Innovation Industry Team. His focus on the healthcare industry provides him with an opportunity to advise businesses and healthcare entities on corporate matters, formation and structuring, contract negotiation, and regulatory compliance. His deep understanding of healthcare operations, billing, and compliance allows for innovative solutions that further coordinate care and strengthen physician alignment. He works with publicly traded and privately owned healthcare entities, including a wide range of not-for-profit organizations.

Chad also advises not-for-profit organizations on governance and policy issues, IRS compliance, and Form 990 issues.

Ryan Grey

Ryan Grey is an associate at Coker. His business valuation background includes business enterprise valuations, purchase price allocations, goodwill impairment testing, stock compensation valuations, and additional audit assist reviews of third-party analyses, using various forms of the income, market, and cost approaches.

Andy Sobcyzk

Andy Sobczyk is a vice president for Coker's physician services and finance, operations, and strategy divisions. Andy joined the Coker team in August 2018 to partner with clients in the ambulatory enterprise arena to deliver value in the areas of operational efficiency, organizational structure, physician alignment strategy due diligence, financial stability, revenue cycle management, and leadership coaching and development. He also supports compensation valuation work, compensation plan redesign, and strategic business planning.

Taylor Cowart

Taylor Cowart is a senior manager with Coker's financial and hospital operations services division. She works predominantly in the provider strategy and physician enterprise arenas, providing clients with consultative assistance for alignment and integration, mergers and acquisitions, provider compensation review and design, service line development, and strategic and tactical planning for health systems and other provider organizations.

Acknowledgments

We would like to express our sincere appreciation to Nancy Collins, Senior Vice President, Content Development and Acquisition, for her instrumental role in bringing Private Equity and Healthcare to the members of the American Association for Physician Leadership. Her publishing efforts and expertise have been invaluable, and it is always a pleasure to collaborate with AAPL to provide relevant information about the healthcare marketplace.

Coker Group also acknowledges the legal expertise of Chad N. Eckhardt, Attorney at Law, Frost Brown Todd LLP, and his legal expertise in the healthcare business environment. Knowledge of healthcare laws and regulations is crucial when entering any Buy/Sell transaction.

Additionally, we express our deep gratitude for all the expertise shown to us first-hand from Coker's new capital partner, Trinity-Hunt Partners of Dallas, Texas, a private equity firm that knows the "right" way of doing such transactions! We truly value their contribution and are appreciative of their support.

Introduction to Private Equity and Healthcare

P*RIVATE EQUITY AND HEALTHCARE* is written in partnership with the American Association for Physician Leadership (AAPL) to offer an objective analysis of the place of private equity (PE) in healthcare. The authors hold no strong position, pro or con, regarding the place of private equity in the healthcare industry. Nonetheless, this topic is of great interest, with hundreds of transactions completed and many more in process or anticipated. These transactions alone justify addressing the many questions surrounding the trend.

PE is embedded into the fiber of healthcare, whether we like it or not, so it deserves careful consideration. Our research and experience show that PE is not for all, but it is for some. Success requires ample financial and operational due diligence and consideration of how physicians work with hospitals and other healthcare providers.

Our view of PE transactions is objective, unbiased, and independent, as is our perspective on how these transactions affect the healthcare provider and payer industry. Therefore, we attempt here to answer many common concerns, including:

- Is PE in healthcare like "mixing oil and water"?
- Can healthcare providers (i.e., hospitals/health systems, physicians of all specialties, advanced practice providers, etc.) co-exist over the long term with overt for-profit investors?
- Is the current PE model workable?
- Will the current PE model be sustained and pass the test of time or is it a passing trend?
- Has the model been tested and proven?
- Will physicians support it in five or 10 years?
- How will hospitals and health systems respond to PE? Can the two co-exist as investors?
- Will medical groups fracture over such transactions?
- Are there state and federal compliance concerns?

- Is PE destined to phase out like physician practice management companies of the 1990s?

These concerns are just a few of the many questions we address in this book.

Ultimately, PE in healthcare will be around for a while. There is too much growth potential and untapped value in this area for it not to be a priority for capital investors seeking value and return.

Further, the changing nature of healthcare delivery for the provider and the organizations they are a part of will only continue to make partnering with PE and PE-backed platforms more attractive. However, it is essential for all parties considering or actively pursuing transactions, whether now or in the future, to be aware of the dynamics involved.

In advising on countless transactions over the years, we have realized that no two deals are the same. Every arrangement has its unique dynamics and characteristics. Nevertheless, two key principles go along with this. First, it is never a pleasant experience to get deep into the deal process, only to be blindsided by something unexpected that could have been, at the very least, anticipated if there had been more familiarity with some of the dynamics we will be discussing.

Second, there are several consistent themes or generalized characteristics that, if one has at least a basic understanding of them, can be foreseen so that those unexpected issues can be avoided or addressed early on in any deal process.

In relating the details of PE transactions, our goal is to inform the reader with an unbiased view of the nature and scope of PE based on our experience advising in numerous buy-well transactions across the industry.

If you are interested in learning more about PEs, whatever your reason, we believe this book will provide you with the information you are looking for.

CHAPTER 1

An Overview of Private Equity and Healthcare

O VER THE LAST FIVE TO 10 YEARS, the growth of private equity (PE) capital investments has, by all measurements, skyrocketed. The topic of PE in healthcare services businesses has dominated many industry conferences, thought leadership perspectives, and media coverage.

PE involvement in the healthcare services sector is not new, however. PE investment funds and PE-backed companies have been involved in this space for decades, and, of course, the industry has never been a stranger to merger and acquisition (M&A) activity, as hospitals and health systems have been engaging in M&A transactions since at least the mid-20th century.

So, what is behind the growth in recent activity and discussion? Jane M. Zhu, MD, MPP, MHSP, of Oregon Health and Science University, says, "In many ways, PE is both a response to and an accelerator of broader health system trends — one in which consolidation is happening quickly, care is being delivered by larger and larger entities, and corporate influence is growing."[1]

DEFINING PRIVATE EQUITY

Private equity, in its simplest form, can be described as any investment in any industry service that does not use public companies or funds. Typically, a consortium of private investors with accumulated personal wealth enlists expert assistance to identify and secure investments in business operations. These capital investments operate only within the guidelines and regulations of private entities.

For any business, including healthcare services, to launch into operation without significant upfront capital is unusual. Traditionally, capital comes from a variety of public and private sources, including foundations, high-net-worth individuals, and endowments from universities and other academic institutions.

HISTORY OF PRIVATE EQUITY IN
THE HEALTHCARE INDUSTRY

The regulatory requirements linked to healthcare services have always been critical in PE transactions. For years, regulatory hurdles have made private capital transactions in healthcare provider entities an obstruction — in many cases, too burdensome to overcome.

Further, it was challenging to paint a clear picture of the economic benefit for those seeking to sink capital (i.e., PE investors). If an investor is going to commit millions — and in some cases hundreds of millions — of dollars, the investor must see a clear return on investment. In addition, the value cases for both investor and seller need to be as understandable as possible.

A primary reason for the recent growth in PE transactions in healthcare is that investors have been more innovative in structuring deals where compelling value can be mapped and navigating the regulatory challenges that previously restricted such deals. Moreover, the industry itself has continued to become more intriguing due to the demographics and recession-resistant nature of the healthcare industry.

Most people understand that while healthcare services come with many regulatory requirements and other barriers unique to this space, such as continuously evolving reimbursement models, provider compensation, technology, and other niche industry dynamics, these services are here to stay. Indeed, due to technological innovation and clinical research, most healthcare areas of specialization are growing at historic rates. As a result, the economic, or value, potential also continues to increase.

Evolution of the System

Private equity in healthcare is not new; however, its emergence has focused more on physician practices and using these practices to build a foundation or platform for aggregating other comparable acquisitions.

There was a time in the healthcare industry when physicians were mostly in private practice, not affiliated through employment or professional services contracts with anyone, much less private equity. The 1990s saw a significant rise in physicians' interest in partnering or affiliating with health systems and hospitals. This trend continues today; most physicians not in private practice are affiliated through employment or some other form of "full" alignment with hospitals and health systems.

Nonetheless, as many health system-physician affiliations have continued, many have soured, even to the point of being undone. In the minds of many, this outcome has left a gap, not only because the transactions dissolved but also due to the general impression that employment is not the best model, possibly not even a workable model. Although private equity investors have addressed this gap, no perfect model exists, including private equity.

As noted in the introduction, this book is not about who is right or wrong relative to physicians (e.g., hospitals, private equity, outside investors, academic institutions, and other affiliation structures); there are valid points supporting every type of relationship, including myriad examples of successes and failures within each model.[2] The intent is not to promote or devalue private equity or any other structural model among healthcare providers. The goal is to provide the facts and education surrounding private equity transactions in the healthcare industry.

There is a role for private equity in healthcare; however, it is essential that the quality of care does not suffer. Nothing is inherently flawed with a for-profit mission, if those participants, including the healthcare providers, do not shortchange patients relative to the quality and delivery of that care. There are many instances where for-profit hospitals and for-profit private equity consortiums have demonstrated how to organize, manage, and efficiently oversee the care of patients without jeopardizing quality.

PRIVATE EQUITY SUCCESSES AND FAILURES

There is a mixed bag of perceived successes or failures in the recent healthcare industry pertaining to outside investor groups. Think back to the 1990s and the rise of physician practice management companies (PPMCs). Although PPMCs were formed and operated for a brief period, not all these investor corporations were private; in many cases, they began as private entities with the prospect that they would soon go public and offer significant returns to their company investors and to the physicians who had "sold out" to the PPMC.

While PPMCs were well established in most cases and offered good management infrastructures, they often failed to create efficiencies and bottom-line profits due to cost savings, reimbursement enhancements, and overall business plan improvements. Further, market variables caused great uncertainty and convolution of performance that led to the demise of many of these entities.

Those who remember the 1990s and the short-lived existence of PPMCs see their similarities in the influence of today's private equity. The fact that PE is met with some degree of skepticism is partly due to its history but also because the basic model and structure that paying for a healthcare entity such as a physician practice with significant upfront dollars via "contrived" compensation reductions is wrought with flaws. Such perceptions as the "physicians will not be as productive as they once were" or "will focus on things other than financial performance" have led to these conclusions.

In addressing these perceptions, the private equity model has been bolstered, and most of these previous flaws have been addressed. Further, the private equity model has done a respectable job of educating the physicians to have realistic expectations post-transaction. Inherent checks and balances ensure that the model will work.

As an example, the rollover equity is significant in providing sufficient incentives for performance so that a future "second bite of the apple," or second chance or opportunity for income, realizes almost as much, if not more, than the first payment.

Private equity arrangements have also done a better job completing due diligence, pre-acquisition education, and analyses to level and synchronize these partner providers; therefore, the private equity model in healthcare is working well as it is currently constructed.

As previously stated, private equity is not for everyone or for every specialty. Some specialties perform and function better within the typical private equity model. Most private equity deals were initially transacted with practice specialties that were not as dependent on or as active in health systems and hospitals. Examples of such specialties include dermatology, ophthalmology, and some hospital-based practices such as anesthesiology, radiology, and pathology.

While some in-hospital work may be necessary, hospitals are neither interested in aligning with these specialties nor do they believe they are required to do so to maintain sufficient working relationships; therefore, these specialties were and remain more attractive to the achievement of transactions with private equity-backed firms.

Over a period of time, private equity proved to be even more successful than initially believed. More specialties that are traditionally aligned with hospitals in both their work and partnering efforts have become of interest to private equity. These include orthopedics, neurosurgery, gastroenterology, urology, and cardiac care specialties. These latter specialties have proved to be challenging competition for private equity deals; these matters will be examined in greater detail to identify the pluses and minuses associated with these situations.

Private equity's relationship with healthcare providers has evolved over recent years, but the beginning of significant involvement by private investor groups in healthcare businesses can be traced back two or three decades. At first, the focus was not solely on physician practices and certain specialties but on an entire consortium of services, which included surgery centers, endoscopy centers, imaging centers, and in some instances, catheterization laboratories.

In recent years, interest in healthcare entities has grown to include physician practices with specific specialties in mind. Not surprisingly, the first specialties targeted were primarily those who were not inclined to practice their specialty in hospitals or those who were not to be of affiliation interest because of their lack of work in hospitals. In other words, hospitals focused on those specialties (e.g., primary care, cardiology, orthopedics, and internal medicine subspecialties), the physicians had greater interest and involvement in working inside of, and for, hospitals.

Looking back again, the 1990s experienced private equity acquisition of assisted living and nursing homes, home health agencies, and related ancillary services, seeking a critical mass of such entities and the prospective ROI that would result. The industry experienced market consolidation and some cost savings, bringing about even greater ROI for the private equity investor groups.

Following these successful efforts, private equity entities began looking for emerging niches such as anesthesiology, radiology, urgent care, and pathology. Later came the acquisition of primary and specialty care outpatient clinics, where much of the focus rests today.

Private equity investors seek a cross-section of services but are often focused and limited to specific specialties. Various private equity funds tied specifically to specialties, such as cardiology and orthopedics, come to mind. (Note: See Chapter 11 for a breakdown of private equity entities by specialties and focus areas.)

Information technology (IT) has also driven private equity investments in healthcare. While most practices and health systems have increased their IT sophistication and services, private equity found opportunities to enhance technology within their entities for growth and expansion. Overall, the potential for private equity to inject significant capital into its model of acquisition or affiliation has and will continue to drive the interest, involvement, and likely success of private equity investors in the healthcare industry.

PRIVATE EQUITY AND ANCILLARY SERVICES

Chapter 8 focuses on ancillaries and private equity transactions, so the topic will not be explored in detail here; however, it is a major driver for such investments. Ancillary services may be the engine that boosts private equity investments, particularly over a longer term and even through subsequent "second bite-of-the-apple" investments. Ambulatory surgery centers lead the way in ancillary investment opportunities.

Private equity funds have little hesitation in investing in the growth of these services, knowing that elective surgeries are considered to be more efficient in an ambulatory setting.[3] This assumes the patient is best served by becoming an inpatient customer and having their surgery outside the hospital operating room (OR).

Other ancillaries cross over every specialty and should be considered within the paradigm of private equity involvement. Accordingly, private equity's investment in ancillaries creates a direct competitive threat to other providers, particularly to hospitals and health systems. This may be the primary reason hospitals and health systems are not proponents of private equity and will do everything possible to limit their involvement. Much of the competition lies within the ancillary services that private equity derives from hospitals and health systems when they align with physician groups.

For example, consider otolaryngology (ENT) practice consortiums. While private equity funds will be attracted to acquire the practice, the real interest is in the surgery centers in which they participate and/or can support a sufficient volume of patients. Surgeries previously performed in an outpatient setting in centers owned by hospitals and health systems are being replaced by private equity capitalized ambulatory surgical centers (ASCs). Given the physicians' involvement in an equity piece of the surgery centers, they become an attractive incentive for aligning with private equity firms.

Although the above conditions are recognized as a formidable obstacle, many examples of successful partnering efforts involve physician groups like ENT, private equity firms, and hospitals and health systems. Three-way joint venture efforts allow for continuity of services but, more importantly, promote a commonality of ownership and ROI among all three entities. Naturally, when three, not two, partners are involved, dilution to a lower percentage of equity results, but with increased efficiencies, better margins, and shared attitudes toward utilization and sources of patients, three-way partnerships have proven successful and are good for the patient.

Therefore, ancillaries will remain a significant part of the private equity continuum of services and overall business plans. Private equity can utilize their vast capital resources to offer more opportunities to physician specialists, but again, hospitals and health systems can have a role in these partnering efforts. In reviewing the various components of private equity transactions and overall perspectives in the healthcare industry, the text will consider in greater detail the areas of review pertaining to ancillary services.

FINANCIAL RAMIFICATIONS OF PRIVATE EQUITY TRANSACTIONS IN HEALTHCARE

In recent years, deal volumes have continued to increase when private equity firms have considered earnings before interest, taxes, depreciation, and amortization (EBITDA) multiples, and overall ROI opportunities in the context of facing more competition for the acquisition of targeted healthcare business entities. That competition comes not only from hospitals and health systems but also from private equity firms where groups are shopping and considering several private equity firms to partner. Thus, the financial makeup of private equity has evolved, becoming more lucrative with the availability of capital. Nonetheless, a market-driven dynamic, that is, the EBITDA derivation, and even more, the multiples of EBITDA derives the initial upfront acquisition.

Rollover percentages have changed, but overall, the complexity of private equity deals continues to increase. For example, many deals include an earnout component in which the physician group has an upside opportunity to realize more proceeds from the sale of their practice in subsequent periods due to specific performance achievements. While earnouts are not common to private equity deals, they are increasing in popularity, particularly for private equity firms and physician groups that see opportunities for upside earnings based on certain tenable performance thresholds.

Multiples of EBITDA will be discussed later, but for now, suffice it to say that they vary with the entity being acquired, the specialty, and the ancillaries that go with or are potential to become a part of the overall services being acquired.

Competition will also dictate the multiples of EBITDA offered. Surgery centers often add to the multiples that would otherwise be lower if they were not a part of the transaction (or even the prospective for future additional surgery centers). Private equity firms now realize that healthcare entities, starting with physician practices, particularly surgical specialties, will provide the ROI they desire. Despite the risk, they have a keen appetite for investment in various private equity acquisitions. For example, Figure 1.1 shows the growth of healthcare transactions by private equity firms since 2001.

While there has been a steady growth of private equity transactions, questions remain about why these firms are so interested in healthcare. Besides the obvious ROI they believe theoretically exists, there are other pros and some cons to consider for whether healthcare is as good an investment for private equity as it seems.

With healthcare's extremely high regulatory environment, this negative factor alone might be significant enough to limit a private equity firm's interest in investments in healthcare. As the U.S. population ages, increased lifetime expectancies, improved technology, and better patient outcomes are all positive factors toward the increased growth of private equity firms' interest in healthcare.

The remaining chapters will continue to examine the pros and cons of private equity investment; however, statistics in Figure 1.1 easily support the premise that private equity and healthcare are well-matched and here to stay.

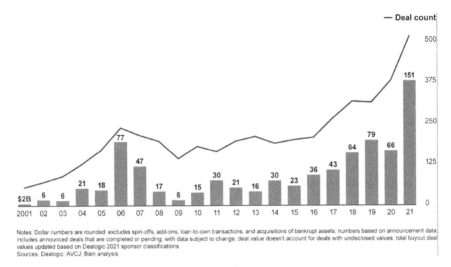

Notes: Dollar numbers are rounded; excludes spin-offs, add-ons, loan-to-own transactions, and acquisitions of bankrupt assets; numbers based on announcement data; includes announced deals that are completed or pending, with data subject to change; deal value doesn't account for deals with undisclosed values; total buyout deal values updated based on Dealogic 2021 sponsor classifications
Sources: Dealogic; AVCJ; Bain analysis

FIGURE 1.1: Global Healthcare Buyout Deal Value

PRIVATE EQUITY AND INVESTMENT RETURN

As with any other venture capitalist, private equity investors expect and deserve a return on their investment. They offer specific models that are sometimes enticing to physicians and sometimes not. The healthcare sector has room for all types of structures and models, as the following chapters will substantiate.

Sometimes, for example, physicians are interested in sizeable upfront dollars, and private equity is essentially the only place where these opportunities remain. Hospitals rarely pay significant amounts at the closing of a transaction; as a result, physicians are less interested, at least those who set goals to achieve upfront dollars from their affiliation structures. Conversely, many physicians, particularly younger ones, place more emphasis on attaining ongoing post-transaction compensation.

Private equity results in an *income scrape*. This, in effect, is a reduction of post-transaction compensation to the physician partners, converting those dollars into earnings before income taxes, depreciation, and amortization (EBITDA), and then capitalizing the value of those dollars based on a multiple of the earnings, which is then largely paid at closing.

However, the result of this calculated formulaic process is, in truth, a reduction in compensation. Created earnings are the result of reduced pay, so those earnings are paid upfront. Private equity investors allow for some *income repair* by offering various levels and components of efficiency and operations improvements, better reimbursement, and other arrangements that allow for a make-up of the lost compensation. If made up, the lost compensation will provide the best of both worlds. The result will be upfront money and, eventually, make-up for a sizable portion of the lost compensation.

Additionally, private equity seeks to ensure that the post-transaction interest among the physician providers continues; a *second bite of the apple is an available opportunity*. This means that part of the sale proceeds, which is usually 100% of the healthcare entity, is reinvested in *rollover equity*.

Rollover equity is typically at least 20% of the entire practice value reinvested. That rollover entity becomes a "Newco," which is the platform upon which the private equity firm aggregates more practices and potentially builds value for that second sale to either another private equity firm or some other venture capitalist. Along with that second sale, the physician investors have the potential to realize a second significant payday without incurring notable risk.

SUMMARY

Deal volumes have increased in number and size. Records have continued to be set for the number of private equity deals in healthcare, largely due to significant available capital ready to be invested by high-wealth, private equity consortiums.

Indeed, private equity's appetite for healthcare transactions has intensified; this worldwide growth includes Europe and Asia Pacific. In later chapters, the alignment of private equity's growth into healthcare, the number, size, and make-up, even very specialty-specific focused private equity funds, which have increased dramatically, will be considered.

Hundreds of funds boasting billions of dollars in assets are available with deals having already been made; substantial capital is ready to invest. Private equity views the somewhat dysfunctional and highly unpredictable U.S. healthcare environment as a "glass-half-full" opportunity while Americans increasingly insist on both high quality and cost containment in their healthcare spending, and state and federal governments are concerned about reducing the cost of their healthcare programs. Thus, private equity will offer an alternative that may help all providers, even health systems and other entities, that perceive private equity investors as competitors, rather than being complementary to their services.

Another opportunity within private equity structures is the power to influence change through innovation and consolidation. Physicians are primarily concerned with the quality of care they provide and in treating their patients. Providing that care in partnership with payers, both governmental and commercial insurance companies, fits with the private equity consortium. In other words, it has a place within our future healthcare provider and payer paradigm.

A common topic is the concern and dissatisfaction pertaining to the current U.S. healthcare system. Many entities are fearful the government will continue to exert its influence and control over the healthcare delivery system, aiming toward a single-payer system sometime soon. Those who find these scenarios onerous, even egregious, will look to private equity firms as a feasible opportunity to invest and inject capital into the companies that will offer better outcomes and patient experiences.

Hospitals, or at least those working under a similar paradigm, share this philosophy and may welcome private equity as a partnership with their medical staff and others. This arrangement could occur even though hospitals see private equity investors as competitors, especially for diagnostic and ancillary service entities.

Those who are a part of that solution and invest in its results will be rewarded for solving the healthcare system's myriad problems. Despite the risks, there is also immense potential for significant returns for private equity investors. Along with meeting legal and ethical boundaries, this movement is healthy for the entire system and should be included in the equation for the future.

Physicians who sell their practices to private equity receive benefits, but they take risks and may face disappointing results. As physicians continue to contend with administrative challenges and stresses, financial issues, regulatory pressures, new payment models, and lower net reimbursement from insurers all emerge as problems that inspire an increased interest in the private equity model.

The major issue of physician burnout, along with a reduced supply of physicians exacerbated by the COVID-19 pandemic, contributes to the interest and viability of private equity. Additionally, hospitals often have limited sources of capital, and private equity is the most logical alternative for responding to that lack of capital when physicians reach out for a partner.

Most physicians still become physicians to practice medicine and find satisfaction in healing their patients' illnesses, injuries, and diseases. Private equity allows the physician that element of independence and autonomy while meeting their financial needs.

Clearly, private equity is here to stay in healthcare. It has its nuances and is unique in structural design and requirements. We will present more specifics and express more candor throughout the chapters of this book; the point to remember is that no model is perfect, nor will there ever be one. Private equity is an option, but it is also imperfect.

REFERENCES

1. Zhu JM. The Growth of Private Equity in US Health Care: Impact and Outlook. NIHCM Foundation. Retrieved Aug 4, 2024, from: https://nihcm.org/publications/the-growth-of-private-equity-in-us-health-care-impact-and-outlook#:~:text=%22In%20many%20ways%2C%20PE%20is,and%20corporate%20influence%20is%20growing.%22

2. Additional information is available in *Affiliation Options for Physicians: Current and Future Strategies* by Max Reiboldt, CPA, which examines virtually all forms of affiliation among healthcare entities, including a basic introduction to private equity. American Association for Physician Leadership; 2020. Available at https://www.physicianleaders.org/publications/books/affiliation-options-for-physicians-current-and-future-strategies?product_name=Affiliation+Options+for+Physicians%3A+Current+and+Future+Strategies

3. Zink C. Ambulatory Surgery Center vs. Outpatient Hospital: Uses, Benefits & More. Verywell health. August 10, 2022. https://www.verywellhealth.com/ambulatory-surgery-center-vs-outpatient-hospital-5498582

CHAPTER 2

Typical Private Equity Healthcare Structures

Private equity (PE)-backed firms' transactional structures are generally similar. The typical setup is based on the acquisition transaction, which is comparable to any other structure when buying another company or legal entity. However, there are unique features of healthcare PE transactions. This chapter explores the typical structures of healthcare entity sales to PE-backed organizations. Note that the terms buyer, purchaser, and investor are used interchangeably.

As in any other transaction of this nature, the purchaser and the seller have their own points of view; however, PE transactions with healthcare entities are unique because the seller is often a physician clinician, and the transactions are subject to many regulatory requirements. Physicians must have a continued interest in the success of the business post-transaction.

INHERENT FEATURES OF PE AND HEALTHCARE TRANSACTIONS

First, we will explore some of the unique features of PE investments. PE is typically structured with an operating entity supported by private investors; their aggregated funds are for common purchases. PE investors are not operators, and even their operating company, which may be a management services organization (MSO), is not always proficient in running the day-to-day operations of a physician practice or other related healthcare businesses. Thus, to ensure successful operations post-transaction, the PE investor requires the seller (often a physician practice comprising several physician partners) to remain fully engaged in the business; otherwise, there will be no interest in purchasing the healthcare entity.

That interest is typically maintained through *rollover equity* and a reinvestment of some of the sale proceeds. The PE management company then seeks and, hopefully, receives legal assurances that those who produce the revenue (typically physicians) will remain with the practice post-transaction (or at least a substantial number will do so with appropriate replacements for those who retire post-transaction), thus assuring that the business will continue to thrive within the capital investment the PE firms intend to make.

PE investors are looking for an appropriate return on their investment from day one, but they are even more concerned about the future when recapitalization of that entity will occur. That recapitalization is in the form of a sale in which the physicians (or other representative sellers) will receive a second return on their investment for that rollover equity (often called the "second bite of the apple").

When a second closing occurs, however, a new capital partner is procured, which means that another PE-backed sponsor will be looking for continued growth and expansion within that practice, along with the aggregated acquired practices that have followed the original platform practice.

With this backdrop, the perspectives of the typical PE purchaser are contrasted with those of the typical PE seller. As basic as this is, it is essential from the outset to understand both sides' perspectives in addition to their overall goals and objectives for completing the transaction.

While some of these goals and objectives of the purchaser and the seller are no different from other buy-sale arrangements of a company in any industry, healthcare transactions have unique features that warrant contemplation as the process continues. The following section presents the most important points a prospective buyer or seller must consider before showing serious interest in completing a transaction.

FEATURES OF TYPICAL PE HEALTHCARE TRANSACTIONS — PURCHASER

Due to the nature of healthcare, especially physician practices, there are unique transaction features that warrant understanding.

PE Operational Entity/Management Organization

As noted previously, the investors comprising PE firms are an amalgamation of high-wealth and high-net-worth consortiums that are (consistent with the name) *private*. They are not publicly traded entities; they are investors who have deliberately chosen to function only in the private sector. While this limits some regulatory requirements and constraints, it does not change many. Moreover, the purchasers' viewpoint is similar in that they require an adequate return on their investment.

Typically, the PE sponsors have formed a management company that is part of the overall PE consortium, but the company is also detached in that they seek and find new acquisitions. When a new company has been acquired, the sponsors complete the integration into the larger platform entity and oversee day-to-day operations to varying degrees based on the sophistication of the management of the company being acquired. (Note: A platform company refers to the initial acquisition made by a private equity group in a specific industry or marketplace. The acquisition is the starting point for other acquisitions in the same industry.) Therefore, the PE investors are removed yet engaged overall in ensuring that the platform and related acquisitions perform to standards.

Purchaser Characteristics

The management entity that the PE sponsors will oversee and control the day-to-day management and administrative oversight. Often, an MSO will be that entity and the PE firm will assume oversight and management of all acquisitions via this administrative infrastructure.

Each platform company, as acquired, will then be considered for subsequent acquisitions to form a larger organization within that specific area of services. For example, the platform company may be a healthcare consulting or advisory firm that will be supported by an aggregation of other companies that perform healthcare professional services.

Capital is funded through the PE sponsors, with those funds applied to acquisitions and corporate overhead of the management company. Each purchase is expected to stand on its own relative to financial performance while continuing to realize significant profits, as was the case prior to the original acquisition platform.

Governance and control over all the PE sponsors continue, but daily operations and management remain with the management company. The PE sponsors are detached from day-to-day management.

The PE sponsors also have majority control of all acquisitions, with only a minority interest in the rollover entity being profitable for the original owners of the businesses acquired. The platform company often will have more equity in the rollover equity than subsequent acquisition sellers that are additions to the platform.

The purchasers (i.e., the management company but, overall, the sponsors) are short-term investors in the sense of their anticipated recapitalization/sale of the platform and related acquisitions within a few years. The time when the capitalization or re-sale occurs depends on several factors, including market conditions, overall financial performance, timing of the sale, and need for capital and expansion, among others.

The PE sponsors are expecting to realize annual profits from both the platform entity and all accretive acquisitions. Nonetheless, there may be low profitability during the acquisition period due to the purchase of additional entities and the required assimilation and integration processes. These are essential to ensure that the platform is performing and that the potential for maximum sales is realized with recapitalization. The PE sponsors approve all acquisitions and related terms and conditions before any deal is finalized.

The operating management entity will have specific responsibilities for that organization. These include a review of purchasing opportunities, consideration of new market possibilities, and overall additions to the platform. Usually, following the acquisition of the platform company there will be an aggressive period when the PE sponsor will provide additional capital and will insist on an aggressive merger and acquisition (M&A) process. This M&A must be added to the platform company; as such, the infrastructures of those acquisitions to the platform and the attainment of "best practices" will be imperative.

The platform company will often have its own M&A team tasked with identifying new acquisitions and consummating the actual deal structure. Daily operations, management, and governance oversight will rest with the management company within the PE-sponsored organization, although the PE-sponsor(s) will not be far removed.

FEATURES OF TYPICAL PE HEALTHCARE TRANSACTIONS — SELLER

From the seller's perspective in a healthcare PE transaction, physicians are often directly involved. While there could be non-physician equity holders in a healthcare entity, especially entities such as an ambulatory surgery center (ASC), imaging centers, and others, it is the physicians who are usually involved. This involvement requires careful consideration relative to the structure of the PE transaction.

For example, if a practice is involved, there will be an inevitable *income scrape*, which results in a reduction in post-transaction compensation. As we explain throughout the book, the income scrape creates the EBITDA (earnings before interest, taxes, depreciation, and amortization) upon which the multiple is then applied to render the value. As such, the physician must fully understand how the process works and be able to handle the reduced compensation post-transaction. Additionally, the typical seller is seeking opportunities to grow and expand with the utilization of the PE sponsor's capital.

This pursuit is logical, and while it could be done by affiliating with the hospital, health system, or another practice group, usually the available capital for growth and expansion is best served by PE. This promotes growth and stability in the practice, even though a majority interest in equity has been relinquished. Nevertheless, this allows for physician-controlled healthcare to have a succession plan, which is often a high priority for older physicians. Conversely, because they are not ready for the income scrape and not in need of a transitional succession plan, younger physicians are not as enamored with the typical PE structure.

Sellers also often look for operational assistance and guidance pertaining to revenue cycle, payer contracting, and overall lack of reimbursement, management, and administrative efficiency. Unless the PE firm acquires a formal MSO with expertise in medical billing and related healthcare matters, many PE firms will be unable to assist the practice with operational efficiency improvements.

Many PE firms are inexperienced in running, managing, and operating medical practices and other healthcare entities; nonetheless, acquiring an MSO does provide some opportunities for operational improvement, guidance, and overall advancement. Sellers should carefully evaluate the operations factor as a viable asset when considering a PE transaction.

As noted, succession planning is often a significant reason for the seller to consider PE. A succession plan is not generally available in health system affiliations because most hospitals do not have the desire or dedicated capital for significant upfront payments. In previous publications, we pointed out a "PE-like" model that responds to PE deal structures for hospitals and health systems.[1] However, this model is unpopular and rarely applied when considering affiliating with hospitals or health systems.

Succession planning, however, is an integral part of the seller's reasons for considering PE. If the younger physicians can be satisfied and their concerns mitigated, the passing on of leadership roles is a viable reason for the practice or other healthcare entity to align with PE.

Sellers must look at their options and consider PE as an alternative to other typical alternatives, such as merging with other practices and affiliating with hospitals. Technically, when a practice affiliates with a hospital via a professional services agreement and not by W-2 employment, it can also be considered a PE affiliation. Nonetheless, hospitals perceive PE as "taking a piece of the overall affiliation pie," which is not best for the long-term working relationship between the hospital and the practice.

Further, ancillaries are enormous economic opportunities for PE, and they are a prerequisite for the transaction with practices. Many of these acquisitions include ancillaries such as ambulatory surgery centers (ASCs) and imaging centers, which must be included to consummate the deal between PE and the seller-owners. Three-way transactions between health systems, PE, the practice, and other healthcare entities are possible and occur regularly. Without their inclusion, a transaction is more challenging and dilutes the equity of each of the parties.

The alternatives to the typical options of affiliating with hospitals and merging with other practices do not prevent PE affiliation (unless the group is fully employed by the hospital or health system), but again, because of ancillaries and other "turf" issues, PE affiliation is difficult for health system transactions, as well.

Payer contracting can be beneficial in working with PE, depending on their overall resources and their aggregation of practices. The challenges of antitrust and trade restrictions are other regulatory issues to consider.

Finally, diversification opportunities come under the broad classification of seller characteristics and interests. Private equity will offer opportunities for diversification in services, products, and ancillaries. Further, it will add other providers, standing locations, and opportunities to work with hospitals and health systems. These factors can be beneficial, but they can create challenges like those outlined above.

SELLER CONSIDERATIONS — EXIT WINDOWS

There are several possibilities for exiting the transaction, although overall, it would be ill-advised for any rollover equity investors to consider an early exit; they will experience a significant discount for an early liquidation of their minority equity investment. Nonetheless, as M&A activity slows, it may be more challenging for investments in PE rollover funds to realize a return; however, overall, more time may be required to complete recapitalization at a multiple EBITDA rate that is acceptable to the majority owner PE sponsors.

Retiring physicians who use the exit window should anticipate this strategy during the completion of the transaction and not learn of it after the fact. Allowances can be made to address their buy-out, albeit at a discount, more favorably than if not considered before the finalization of the transaction.

Retiring physicians who utilize an exit window usually see discounted valuations, the amount of which could be better negotiated if known before the transaction consummation. Whenever a liquidation is anticipated before the actual point that all the investors, including the majority owner PE sponsor, want it to happen, it is much better than completing it before this time.

Since the discount amount could be significant, it is better that it be bought out by the practice than to wait for the recap or to convince the PE firm to agree for him to continue to hold his equity via the rollover and wait for the recap to occur years later. If possible, these matters should be worked out prior to the PE transaction.

At the outset, the seller representatives should know and consider the economic terms and conditions of the PE healthcare entity transaction. Being aware that although the terms may seem obvious, the information may not be clearly defined forces the physicians to negotiate a better rate after the transaction, which is highly improbable for success (i.e., generate a higher price for an early exit).

Sometimes, the novice investor finds it difficult to understand all the confusing terms and nuances involved within the transaction relative to the economic structure. Appendix D is a glossary of frequently used terms unique to PE deals. Although some terms are general and not exclusive to PE deals, they are still relevant.

It is also the responsibility of the sell-side advisor to ensure that the non-deal-making client (usually physicians) fully understands the meaning of these terms and especially how the meaning affects the actual transaction. The transaction should contain no surprises before, during, or post-closing as work is done regarding the overall structural parameters.

Another point that all parties should understand is that when a practice is sold to a PE entity, the sellers are no longer the majority owners. Discussions before closing should define the extent to which the seller will continue to be involved in governance, leadership, and voting. The sellers must understand that they are giving up majority control and no longer have the license or the legal right to make decisions that would now rightfully be those of the new majority owner. Collaboration is still necessary although the majority owner controls the decisions.

In recent years, the consideration of environmental, social, and governance matters (ESG) in post-transaction operations and investment practices has arisen. While these matters have been a priority for public companies, the PE sector has more recently experienced emphasis on ESG as well; many PE firms have dedicated ESG specialists, usually within the management company, to support those efforts with the minority sellers/owners. The adoption of ESG practices and initiatives throughout the PE sector is becoming a critical matter that may also be identified within the due diligence period, before the closing, with more documentation on the entity's internal ESG functionality and expertise.

Before the transaction closes, the seller should be aware of other relational and cultural considerations, with their advisory firm directing focus on these areas of concern. Often, we speak about culture and how it must be protected post-transaction to help the PE firm realize the maximum return on investment (ROI), but this issue can be overplayed, especially by the seller.

Remember that, good, bad, or indifferent, the PE sponsor is primarily looking for an acceptable ROI, an adequate economic return. This objective is not always consistent with physicians' perspectives, which are first focused on quality of care and overall efficiencies to support that aim.

We do not infer that PE sponsors are uncaring or have a lesser view of the importance of quality of care to patients; their initial motivation, nevertheless, is the investment return. When entering a PE transaction, the sellers must consider this economic reality and deal with it accordingly, or they should not proceed with the transaction.

HEALTHCARE REGULATORY CONSIDERATIONS

We would be remiss in addressing the key elements of PE transactions without mentioning the healthcare regulatory boundaries governing healthcare entities. We cover regulation matters in more depth in other chapters, specifically in Chapter 3. While it is true that such transactions among PE investor sponsors and healthcare providers are not subjected to the high degree of regulations and compliance requirements of health systems and physician providers, many restrictions apply.

For example, areas of compliance include the following:

- Restrictive covenants and non-compete agreements.
- Antitrust and Federal Trade Commission regulations.
- Fraud and abuse structures between physician providers.
- Issues concerning cybersecurity and ransomware attacks.
- Privacy regulations, including the Health Insurance Portability and Accountability Act (HIPAA) laws.
- Implementation of the No Surprises Act (NSA).
- Regulatory requirements apply and must be considered a significant part of any PE healthcare-related entity transaction.

OVERALL GOALS AND OBJECTIVES

In summary, when pondering typical PE structures among healthcare providers and PE investors, it is appropriate to consider several goals and objectives and realize that some are top priorities when pursuing such transactions.

First is the economic ROI. Both the seller and the purchaser require a certain return, or the deal will be terminated prematurely and no additional aggregated transactions to the platform will result. The amount of economic ROI expected may vary, but the PE sponsors require a return that will be at least a percentage in the teens and often much more.

A strategic and tactical plan for both the seller and the purchaser should be drawn up. While this action seems elementary, putting it into the context of an actual transaction can be challenging to quantify. A strategic plan for a practice can be quite different from that of a PE sponsor, although there is some commonality. A tactical plan addressing such matters for both the seller and the buyer will be similar to the strategic plan; the plan should consider both strategy and tactics while establishing specific goals and objectives.

A PE firm's seller is looking for a capital partner. In many ways, this is no different from merging with another larger group or affiliating closely through employment or a professional service agreement (PSA) with a health system. That seller and the selected partner will mutually benefit from a solid strategic and tactical plan, as discussed, with the result being a favorable economic ROI.

Responding to industry trends, challenges, stresses, strengths, weaknesses, and other measures is also a significant part of the goals and objectives of both the seller and the buyer in PE transactions. Protecting and nurturing stability and long-term viability is a significant part of a suitable response.

Another objective is simply making the most of the transaction within a vibrant and viable healthcare industry structure; taking a capital partner and realizing better ROI is indeed a worthwhile initiative.

SUMMARY

Allowing private investors to provide benefits to industry participants (e.g., physicians and other healthcare providers) and allowing those private investors to realize financial gain while benefitting the providers as well, are all admirable goals and objectives for both the seller and the buyer.

Competitive alternatives via PE deals are also worth consideration within a PE healthcare transaction's overall goals and objectives. Physicians often say they are not businesspeople, that their primary interest is caring for and healing their patients; although this is true, having a capital/strategic partner can fill a financial void.

Finally, the objective of regulatory compliance and legitimate, legally established, and structured economic gain is a worthwhile benefit.

As we have in this chapter, we will continue to explore the nuances of PE considerations fairly and without prejudice, as we have considered the basis of these structures. More unbiased details and other characteristics of PE and healthcare transactions follow.

REFERENCE

1. Reiboldt M. *Affiliation Options for Physicians. Washington, DC:* American Association for Physician Leadership, 2020.

CHAPTER 3

Healthcare Laws Impacting Private Equity Transactions

GOING BACK TO THE HIPPOCRATIC OATH, written between the 5th and 3rd centuries BC, the practice of medicine has been held in high esteem with correspondingly high ethical standards. Many considerations that prompted such high regard for the medical profession also underline the robust legal and regulatory framework in which modern healthcare must operate.

Not only are physicians, nurses, and other practitioners held to high levels of educational excellence and individual responsibility, corporate entities that operate within the healthcare industry are also held to similarly high legal standards.

While investors in private equity funds increasingly focus attention and investment in myriad opportunities within the healthcare industry, such as pharmaceuticals and medical equipment, they have also poured significant investment into medical practices within the past 15 years.

Given the historically fragmented industry of medical practices and economic opportunities for selling physicians, private equity (PE) funds have begun to invest heavily in specific specialties. However enticing this space has become, investments come with risk that is unique to not just the healthcare industry, but also the practice of medicine.

This chapter focuses on the general regulatory framework applicable to private equity investments in healthcare practices. Additional discussion is offered regarding common practices that develop business operations that comply with key legal requirements such as the corporate practice of medicine doctrine, antitrust, anti-kickback, the physician self-referral law, and the false claims act.

CORPORATE PRACTICE OF MEDICINE

Traditionally, medical practices were small and owned by the physicians who treated the patients. Today, private investors are increasingly interested in creating and developing financial ties to or purchasing equity interest in physician practices. The healthcare industry has seen the consolidation of many physicians into larger practices as the market adapts to the influence of these investors.

The patient-physician relationship and the physician's ability to use unrestricted judgment are essential to healthcare. Many states have enacted corporate practice of medicine (CPOM) laws to keep the patient-physician relationship insulated from corporate influences. CPOM laws recognize that a corporation's obligation to its shareholders may not always align with the physicians' to their patients and may interfere with a physician's professional judgment. The laws represent the principle that physicians should make patient care decisions using their own independent professional judgment.

Generally, CPOM laws prevent non-physicians and non-physician-owned business entities from influencing patient care by prohibiting corporations from practicing medicine or employing physicians to provide professional medical services.

States vary in how they enforce the prohibition of unlicensed individuals practicing medicine. While some states explicitly require medicine to be practiced through particular corporate forms, other states simply rely on case law, which developed the prohibition based on the statutory requirement that one must have a license to practice medicine.

Because physicians are licensed by individual states, the right to practice and compliance requirements for business entities supporting the practice of medicine vary significantly from state to state.

To add to the complexity, the CPOM doctrine in each state consists of more than statutory enactments. Regulations, case law, opinions from the attorney general, and opinions from medical licensing boards create a more nuanced body of law that provides more guidance on what exactly is required, allowed, and prohibited.[1]

Finally, CPOM laws are not limited to physicians and can apply to a wide variety of professionals licensed in many different fields within the industry, including dentistry, optometry, physical therapy, speech therapy, chiropractic, and many others. Although CPOM laws address significant public policy concerns, excluding outside investors limits opportunities that have become commonplace in other industries. One common method of permitting outside entities' involvement in medical practices without violating CPOM rules is by using a management services organization (MSO).

MSOs are business entities that, as the name suggests, provide management and administrative services to professional entities, which remain entirely owned by the relevant appropriately licensed providers. Typically, MSOs are controlled by unlicensed individuals.

Please note that most states allow the MSO to be formed under any business structure recognized by that state. Concerning the medical practice, however, many states require that entity to be formed as a professional corporation or a professional services corporation. Some states allow professional limited liability companies, professional associations, or professional limited liability partnerships.

The professional entity and MSO enter a contract that binds them in a business venture, each with distinct responsibilities. The professional entity controls the clinical, healthcare-related functions such as providing medical services, hiring and firing licensed professionals, and receiving funds generated from the professional services. The MSO provides nonclinical services such as leasing space and equipment, marketing, and ensuring regulatory compliance, among other necessary administrative functions.

The professional entity pays the MSO for providing business services through a management fee determined in their contract. When creating the contract, the parties must carefully consider the fees charged for services rendered by the MSO because states often have fee-splitting laws in place to ensure physicians remain in control of medical decision making. These laws generally mandate that a provider should not split patient fees between licensed and unlicensed individuals, except in certain circumstances.

For example, in certain states, the management fee cannot be a percentage of the practice's receivables. In those states, the professional entity and MSO may contract for a flat fee, which represents the fair market value (FMV) of the management services provided.

When considering an MSO model, physicians should balance the benefits of the business plan against the liabilities. An MSO can remove the administrative burden off physicians' shoulders, allowing them to focus on patient care. On the other hand, a poorly structured MSO may increase a practice's legal and financial risk.

ANTITRUST CONSIDERATIONS

Private equity investors and counsel also must analyze their transactions and business structure for antitrust compliance. This is especially true under the Biden administration which has been prompting the Federal Trade Commission (FTC) and the Department of Justice (DOJ) to scrutinize healthcare consolidations and joint ventures more closely as a means of ensuring healthy competition with the goal of reducing the overall cost of healthcare.

After such prompting, the unique development of private equity transactions in the healthcare market brought the private equity industry front and center. The FTC tends to focus on insurance, pharmaceuticals, and consumer protection issues, whereas the DOJ focuses on mergers. To make matters more interesting, states are becoming increasingly involved in healthcare antitrust regulation through their attorneys general. Regulating agencies consider factors such as market consolidation, barriers to entry, and effects on pricing when reviewing transactions.

Consumers benefit from competitive healthcare markets because the costs are lower and the care is better. On the other hand, rampant consolidation and anticompetitive practices often result in reduced quality and increased cost of care. Monopoly or near-monopoly control in certain industries or practices can lead to increased rates with insurers, which are ultimately passed down to the patients in increased premiums, copays, and coinsurance.

Government agencies are concerned about transactions to the extent they focus on short-term gains, aggressive cost-cutting, or decrease competition. Healthcare workers in systems affected by consolidation and acquisitions reported "fewer caregivers, degradation of care, commoditization of health care services, and increased prices."[2]

In a statement regarding private equity investing, FTC Commissioner Chopra expressed concerns about private equity investing in the opioid treatment, hospice, and air ambulance sectors. The commissioner explained that the loss of competition was not the only troubling aspect in these investments; surprise medical billing and body brokering were among the acquisition strategies that result in higher costs and reduced quality of care. Congress addressed these specific considerations in 2021 with the enactment of the No Suprises Act and Eliminating Kickbacks in Recovery Act, which are discussed in Appendix C.

The Hart-Scott-Rodino (HSR) Act established the federal pre-merger notification program.[3] Parties to mergers or acquisitions meeting the filing threshold must provide the FTC and DOJ with information regarding each party's business and the proposed deal. The parties then wait while enforcement agencies review the transaction. The filing threshold required for transactions closing on or after March 6, 2024, has increased to $119.5 million.[4]

Yet, some deals in the healthcare sector have been scrutinized for antitrust violations even though the deal may fall below the HSR reporting threshold. A possible explanation for this scrutiny is that these enforcement agencies have become aware of and sensitive to private equity investments in healthcare. Certain acquisitions can lead to the consolidation of certain markets, which can stifle competition or result in aggressive cost-cutting measures.

On March 5, 2024, the FTC hosted a public workshop and was joined by the leaders from the DOJ, the Department of Health and Human Services (HHS), and the Centers for Medicare and Medicaid Services (CMS).[5] These government agencies reaffirmed their commitment to protect the healthcare market and patients from private equity practices that they viewed as harmful to patients and the industry.

The agencies announced they were paying close attention to certain practices which they believe may undercut long-term growth and create misaligned financial incentives.

1. One of these practices is short-term ownership or "flip-and-strip" approaches, in which a private equity firm takes on a large amount of debt to acquire a healthcare entity, increases the profits quickly, and sells it shortly after.

2. The agencies announced concerns with the private acquisition of emergency rooms, as more than 40% of ERs in the country are overseen by private equity firms.

3. "Cut-and-run" approaches were declared a concern because the firms can sell the healthcare entity after extreme cuts fail to produce desired profits.

4. Roll-ups were viewed as a cause for concern because firms can acquire and consolidate large shares of the market power by making small, non-HSR reportable acquisitions.

5. "Cross-ownership" was flagged because under this approach, firms buy significant shares in rivals firms competing in the industry, which softens the incentives to compete.

6. Obscure corporate structures motivated the agencies to declare a commitment to conducting oversight to increase transparency regarding ownership of entities owned by private equity firms.

States also have increasingly become involved in scrutinizing acquisitions in the healthcare sector. States are enacting laws modeled after the federal HSR to be able to review transactions that fall below the federal reporting threshold. These laws, commonly referred to as "mini-HSRs" or "Baby HSRs," may require companies to file state pre-merger notifications under certain circumstances that would not require notification under federal rules. California, Colorado, Connecticut, Hawaii, Illinois, Massachusetts, Minnesota, Nevada, New Hampshire, New York, Oregon, Rhode Island, and Washington have already implemented such laws.

One important consideration for private equity investors regarding the Baby HSRs is the standard the state uses to apply the law. For example, some states are concerned with competition and antitrust issues; other states are concerned with the impact the merger might have on the public, making it difficult to conduct a risk assessment on a broader scale. The cost of conducting reviews to ensure compliance under the Baby HSRs may kill some smaller transactions.

Although federal enforcement agencies have pledged to scrutinize private equity firms, they have not yet been able to celebrate clean-cut successes. For example, the FTC sued to enjoin private equity firm Welsh Carson and its portfolio company, U.S. Anesthesia Partners (USAP). The FTC alleged both entities are violating or will violate antitrust laws for monopolizing the anesthesia market in Texas.[6] Interestingly, the Southern District of Texas granted Welsh Carson's motion to dismiss but denied USAP's motion to dismiss.

The court dismissed Welsh Carson because it was not violating antitrust laws. The court held that receiving profits from USAP was not an ongoing violation because profits, sales, and other benefits resulting from an initial wrongdoing are not treated as an independent act. Moreover, the court held that owning noncontrolling, minority interests in a healthcare company is not an ongoing violation of antitrust laws.

Second, the court dismissed the private equity firm because it was not about to violate antitrust laws. The FTC argued that Welsh Caron had already orchestrated a monopoly and had the blueprint in place to do it again, yet the court reasoned that the mere capacity to do something does not mean it is likely to occur. While USAP still exists and, allegedly, consolidates the anesthesiology market and stifles competition, the court limited responsibility for these actions at the portfolio company level.

On the other hand, the court reasoned it was premature to dismiss claims against the anesthesiology practice. The FTC alleged USAP continues to own anesthesia groups unlawfully acquired, engages in price-setting agreements, retains monopolization schemes, and maintains assets of acquisitions that plausibly contribute to the monopoly power.

This case is still unfolding, but USAP is already a cautionary tale to physicians and professional entities. Investors and professional entities should consider both antitrust concerns in their deal strategy. Counsel can help structure transactions to avoid or mitigate the risk that may result in scrutiny from these regulatory agencies. Especially in an industry facing heightened scrutiny from an evolving set of regulations, retaining counsel to structure and guide private equity investments may be the key to surviving regulatory review.

THE ANTI-KICKBACK STATUTE

Private equity firms looking to expand into healthcare must be wary of violating three federal laws that carry potential civil and criminal penalties. The first law we will discuss is the federal Anti-Kickback Statute or AKS.

The AKS, 42 U.S.C. 1320a- 7b(b), prevents anyone, including physicians, healthcare providers, and healthcare suppliers, from receiving remuneration for referring patients to another physician, healthcare provider, or healthcare supplier when that patient is covered by a federal healthcare program such as Medicare or Medicaid.

While the term "referring" sounds simple, a referral does not have to take the form of a written note providing an explicit recommendation that a patient seek the services of another healthcare provider, physician, or supplier.

Courts have interpreted referral under the AKS to include requests by a physician for a consultation with another physician, requests or establishment of a plan of care by a physician that includes the provision of health services, and the certifying or recertifying of the need for any health service for which payment may be made under a federal healthcare service.

Private equity firms that acquire a physician practice or healthcare-providing entity may be held liable for the actions of a physician or healthcare provider that violate the AKS, even if the physician is not found liable. However, there are some significant limitations to liability regarding the referrals.

Because of its criminal structure, the AKS requires knowledge of and intent to commit a violation; however, knowledge and intent can be shown if the private equity firm acts with intentional ignorance as to the practices or recklessly disregards such a risk. Therefore, there is a fine line between disregarding AKS risk and claiming lack of knowledge as a defense against AKS violations.

The AKS requires that a referral be made and that remuneration be paid for the referral. Remuneration is the receipt of anything of value in exchange for a referral, such as payment of money, payment of rent, new equipment, or even the performance of services.

Given the breadth of the AKS' application, the Office of Inspector General (OIG) for the Department of Health and Human Services who enforces the AKS has promulgated a number of safe harbors. The safe harbors are an extensive list of permissible arrangements that will be immune from scrutiny, if properly satisfied. The list includes many arrangements, including the following, which are commonly applicable to private equity investment in medical practices:

1. Returns on investment interests
2. Space rental
3. Equipment rental
4. Sale of a practice, and
5. Personal services and management contracts[7]

An element of nearly every safe harbor is that the compensation provided to the party in a position to make referrals is consistent with fair market value (FMV) and not structured in a way in which it considers, directly or indirectly, the volume or value of referrals or other business generated between the parties. While valuations by independent and objective third parties are helpful to evidence the intent to comply with this common element, such valuations do not provide automatic protection.

For private equity firms transacting business in the healthcare field, it is important to understand that the AKS imposes criminal liability. Thus, a violation of the law could result in fines up to $50,000 per kickback and three times the amount of remuneration provided, imprisonment for up to 10 years, and exclusion from federal healthcare program participation. Consequently, no federal healthcare program payment may be made for any items or services furnished, directly or indirectly, by an excluded person or at the medical direction or on prescription of an excluded person.

Violation of such an exclusion may result in a civil monetary penalty of $10,000 for each claimed item or service furnished during the period that the person or entity was excluded, and the excluded person or entity may be subject to an assessment of up to three times the amount claimed for each item or service.

THE PHYSICIAN SELF-REFERRAL LAW (STARK LAW)

The Physician Self-Referral Law, Section 1877 of the Social Security Act (42 U.S.C. 1395nn), commonly called the Stark Law, prohibits a physician from making referrals of designated health services payable by Medicare and Medicaid[1] to an entity with which the physician or an immediate family member has a financial relationship unless an exception is met. The law also prohibits filing claims with Medicare for any improperly referred designated healthcare services.

While the initial designated health service (DHS) was clinical laboratory services, the list has grown through the years. The current DHS categories are as follows:

1. Clinical laboratory services
2. Physical therapy services
3. Occupational therapy services
4. Outpatient speech-language pathology services
5. Radiology and certain other imaging services
6. Radiation therapy services and supplies
7. Durable medical equipment and supplies
8. Parental and enteral nutrients, equipment
9. Prosthetics, orthotics, and prosthetic devices and supplies
10. Home health services

11. Outpatient prescription drugs
12. Inpatient and outpatient hospital services

The first six designated health services listed above are defined by the Code List provided on the List of CPT/HCPCS Codes | CMS. The remaining six DHS categories are defined at 42 CFR 411.351 without reference to the Code List. Given the complexity of billing for medical services and supplies provided, it is essential to have a clear understanding of what constitutes DHS for purposes of compliance with the Stark Law.

The Stark Law is a strict liability statute, meaning the government need not show intent to violate the law to hold physicians accountable for these violations. The best way to avoid liability for violations of the Stark Law is to make use of one or more of the established exceptions. Some examples of exceptions that are commonly applicable to private equity arrangements in healthcare include:

- Rental of Office Space. This exception generally requires that the lease arrangement be (1) for at least one year in duration, (2) set out in writing, (3) signed by the parties, and (4) specify the premises covered. Rent payments must be at FMV and not determined in a way that considers the volume or value of referrals or other business generated between the parties.
- Rental of Equipment. This exception generally allows payments to be made by the lessee to a lessor for the use of equipment so long as the lease arrangement is (1) set out in writing, (2) signed by the parties, and (3) specifies the equipment covered. Rent payments must be at FMV and not determined in a manner that considers the volume or value of referrals or other business generated between the parties. Any "per-click," or "per-use" payment arrangement may be prohibited.
- Bona fide Employment Relationships. This exception generally allows an employer to make payments to a physician who has a bona fide employment relationship with the employer for the provision of services if (1) the employment is for identifiable services, (2) the amount of remuneration under employment is consistent with fair market value of services and is not determined in a manner that takes into account the volume or value of referrals by the referring physician, and (3) the remuneration is provided under an arrangement that

would be commercially reasonable even if no referrals were made to the employer.

Additional exceptions have been developed for personal services contracts, fair market value arrangements, in-office ancillary services, and others. Each exception is unique and typically involves the use of numerous defined terms and key concepts.[7]

The Stark Law exceptions are particularly important for private equity firms. Unlike the AKS safe harbors, which guarantee that an action is legal but do not guarantee that actions falling outside of the safe harbors are illegal, the exceptions to the Stark Law are truly exceptions. Any arrangement that implicates the Stark Law and does not fit within an applicable exception is a violation of the law and a potential liability for the private equity firm that owns the business to address.

Violation of the Stark Law may result in potentially devastating sanctions and civil liability.

1. No matter the intent of the violating party, no payment shall be given for an arrangement that violates the Stark Law, so the service would be provided at the expense of the healthcare provider.
2. If the violator knows or should have known that an improper claim was submitted then that violator shall be subject to a civil penalty of up to $15,000 for each service.
3. If the violator entered an arrangement for which the violator knows or should have known that the principal purpose was ensuring referrals by a physician in violation of the Stark Law, then the violator shall be subject to civil penalty of up to $100,000 for each arrangement.

Private equity firms buying or investing in physician-owned groups, hospitals, or other healthcare businesses should ensure that if referrals are made, they are done so within the context of the exceptions to the Stark Law.

THE FALSE CLAIMS ACT

The False Claim Act (FCA) allows the government to recover money when someone submits a false or fraudulent claim for payment to the government. These claims may be for Medicare and Medicaid, and the extent of the claim can be as grand as a claim of service rendered to the patient that was never provided or as slight as services that were provided were unsupported by the patient's medical record.

The FCA is particularly unique in that it allows for *qui tam* claims, or claims filed by private individuals on behalf of the government. In the context of the FCA, this means that individuals can sue a private equity firm as the owner of a physician group if the person bringing suit believes that the private equity firm directly, or the physician group the private equity firm owns, is defrauding the government by submitting claims of fabricated medical procedures to Medicare or Medicaid.

When a *qui tam* claim is pursued, the government is listed as the plaintiff; however, the individual who brought the claim is incentivized to do so as the individual is entitled to an award of a percentage of the money recovered by the government, generally 15%–30%.

Therefore, one of the greatest risk factors for private equity firms in the healthcare field is a lawsuit from a current or former member of a physician group that the private equity firm owns. Unlike the private equity firm, these individuals have far more intimate knowledge of the operations of the medical practice; however, under the FCA, they are able to allege that the private equity firm as the majority owner of the business was involved enough in the claims to be liable.

As such, one of the best ways for private equity firms to avoid FCA litigation is by fostering a culture of compliance within the practices the firm is invested in. This means encouraging regulatory compliance and disseminating knowledge throughout the business owned by the firm.

The OIG has developed supplemental guidance for an effective compliance program at medical practices. This document provides an invaluable resource to private equity firms that are developing a compliance program and considering how to make such a program truly effective. Compliance guidance tools are available at https://oig.hhs.gov/compliance/compliance-guidance/.

The risk of a former employee bringing a *qui tam* claim can be mitigated by ensuring that the culture of the business is not only compliant legally but that employees are given no reason to hold a vendetta against the firm or its leadership to the point of acting in retaliation.

When the government or an individual suing on its behalf brings an FCA claim, the pleading must be done with particularity. Specifically, the plaintiff must allege that the defendant knowingly presented or caused to be presented to an officer or employee of the United States government, a false or fraudulent claim for payment or approval. The key elements from this analysis are knowingly, caused, presented, false or fraudulent, and officer or employee of the U.S. government.

If a plaintiff alleges that a physician at a clinic owned by the private equity firm submitted a false claim but the private equity firm had no involvement was not involved whatsoever in the process, then it is unlikely that such a claim would stand unless the plaintiff can demonstrate that knowledge should be inferred against the private equity firm due to deliberate ignorance or reckless disregard.

When the government pursues a violation of the False Claims Act, the government must demonstrate that the provider knew or should have known that the claims were false when submitted. Similar to the AKS, this knowledge requirement can be imputed onto the private equity firm for the actions of physicians in the business owned by the private equity firm. This depends on whether the private equity firm was so involved in the management of the practice that it should have known about the submission of false claims, or where the private equity firm is willfully ignorant as to the fraudulent submission of claims when it had reason to believe such claims were being submitted.

Violation of the False Claims Act can see a service provider fined up to three times the program's loss, plus an additional $11,000 per claim, which, adjusted for inflation, is $27,894 in 2024. Such per-claim penalties can be crippling, especially if the violation is systemic. Further, violations of AKS or Stark can serve as the basis for FCA violations.

Additionally, the Affordable Care Act created an obligation for healthcare providers to report and return overpayments they received within 60 days of identifying such overpayments. Failure to do so results in each overpayment becoming an obligation for the purposes of the False Claims Act.

Private equity firms must mitigate risk through strong internal governance systems and corporate structures. Unlike the AKS, which has safe harbors, or The Physician Self-Referral Laws which are particular to DHS, the False Claims Act is far broader, and the potential for *qui tam* claims makes the False Claims Act a particularly dangerous law for private equity firms.

LOPER BRIGHT ENTERPRISES V. RAIMONDO

It's important to note that the laws affecting private equity transactions in healthcare have been largely based on the opinions of administrations/agencies, such as the Office of the Inspector General of the Department of Health and Human Services. It is important to note that the laws affecting private equity transactions in healthcare have been largely based on the opinions of administrations/agencies, such as the Office of the Inspector General of the Department of Health and Human Services.

Previously, under *Chevron U.S.A., Inc. v. Natural Resources Defense Council, Inc.,* courts were required to defer to these administrative/agency decisions when there was an ambiguity within the statute that required some judicial interpretation.

Chevron, however, was recently overturned by the Supreme Court of the United States' decision in *Loper Bright Enterprises v. Raimondo*. In this case, the Court found that the power to interpret the law lies solely with the judiciary and that courts are not required to rely on the opinions of federal administrations, even if the administration was formed specifically due to the elevated level of knowledge needed to regulate that area of the law.

The full impact of this decision is still unfolding, and it remains to be seen how courts will apply this new ruling. The medical profession has long been the subject of extensive regulation and administrative authority; therefore, the way in which laws like the Anti-Kickback Statute or the Stark Law are applied could change drastically, or courts could willingly continue to apply these laws the same way they were applied before *Chevron* was overturned.

The important thing for private equity firms to keep in mind is that this is a time of uncertainty; the laws discussed above could become less restrictive under the full authority of the courts, or courts could interpret the laws more strictly than they were viewed under the CMS and OIG opinions.

SUMMARY

Antitrust and corporate practice of medicine laws require careful structuring and complicated contractual arrangements, which, in turn, bring in the laws described above.

The AKS provides safe harbors within which to fit arrangements to ensure they do not violate the law. However, just because an arrangement does not squarely fit within a safe harbor does not mean that the arrangement violates the AKS. On the other hand, The Physician Self-Referral Law (Stark Law) provides minimal exceptions, allowing arrangements that would otherwise violate the Stark Law. Identifying these risks and proceeding cautiously in an uncertain time in the law is essential to guarantee the continued success of private equity investments in healthcare.

During this time of regulatory uncertainty, private equity firms may benefit by their operating entities engaging separate legal counsel with a particularized understanding of the law. Doing so also maintains corporate separation.

REFERENCES

1. American Medical Association. *Issue brief: Corporate Practice of Medicine*. American Medical Association. 2015. Accessed June 11, 2024. https://www.ama-assn.org/sites/ama-assn.org/files/corp/media-browser/premium/arc/corporate-practice-of-medicine-issue-brief_1.pdf

2. U.S. Department of Justice. Deputy Assistant Attorney General Andrew Forman Delivers Keynote at ABA's Antitrust in Healthcare Conference. U.S. Department of Justice Office of Public Affairs. June 3, 2022. Accessed August 6, 2024. https://www.justice.gov/opa/speech/deputy-assistant-attorney-general-andrew-forman-delivers-keynote-abas-antitrust. https://www.justice.gov/opa/speech/deputy-assistant-attorney-general-andrew-forman-delivers-keynote-abas-antitrust.

3. Federal Trade Commission. Premerger Notification Program. Federal Trade Commission. Accessed August 6, 2024. https://www.ftc.gov/enforcement/premerger-notification-program#:~:text=The%20Hart-Scott-Rodino%20Act%20established%20the%20federal%20premerger%20notification,submit%20premerger%20notification%20to%20the%20FTC%20and%20DOJ.

4. Federal Trade Commission. New HSR Thresholds and Filing Fees for 2024. Federal Trade Commission. February 5, 2024. Accessed August 6, 2024. https://www.ftc.gov/enforcement/competition-matters/2024/02/new-hsr-thresholds-filing-fees-2024.

5. Federal Trade Commission. Remarks by Chair Lina M. Khan As Prepared for Delivery Private Capital, Public Impact Workshop on Private Equity in Healthcare. Federal Trade Commission Public Statement. March 5, 2024. Accessed August 6, 2024. https://www.ftc.gov/news-events/news/speeches/remarks-chair-lina-m-khan-prepared-delivery-private-capital-public-impact-workshop-private-equity

6. *Federal Trade Commission v. U.S. Anesthesia Partners, Inc. et al, No. 4:2023cv03560 – Document 146 (S.D. Tex. 2024)*. Justia. Accessed June 11, 2024. https://law.justia.com/cases/federal/district-courts/texas/txsdce/4:2023cv03560/1935515/146/.

7. National Archives. Code of Federal Regulations. Exceptions to the Referral Prohibition Related to Compensation Arrangements. Accessed June 11, 2024. https://www.ecfr.gov/current/title-42/chapter-IV/subchapter-B/part-411/subpart-J/section-411.357

CHAPTER 4

Valuation and Quality of Earnings in Private Equity Transactions

E CONOMIC VALUATION WITHIN PRIVATE EQUITY inevitably is questioned early in the private equity (PE) transaction process. Valuation is a significant part of the decision-making process for the buyer and the seller and, as a result, entails a defined process. While simple in theory, this process work in a PE model involves concerted technical review, modeling, and futuristic economic performance assumptions relative to the healthcare entity under consideration. This undertaking is often completed by outside parties independent of the buyer or the seller yet engaged and paid for by either or both.

The valuation review usually takes on a broader quality of earnings (QofE) process. Regardless, it results from a third-party expert independently engaged by either buyer or seller and their conclusions drawn.

ENTERPRISE VALUE

The goal of the valuation and QofE process is to independently assess and derive *enterprise value* of the entire aggregated entity under consideration. The processes considered and completed within the independent analyses should relate to the final decision and the purchase price for the business. After enterprise value is derived, the reinvestment in the rollover entity is completed but usually is based on the overall enterprise value and whatever percentage of that sales amount is carved out and dedicated to the reinvestment, usually 20%–30%.

Certain overarching principles guide the determination of enterprise value. First, the independent valuator must understand and quantify the compensation income scrape or "haircut," which is a reduction in physicians' compensation after a practice is sold to a private equity firm. This compensation reduction should be applied to physicians who by ownership are part of the sale of the practice or other healthcare entity. Once that scrape is determined, additional financial analyses are completed within a pro forma financial modeling process with the goal *of normalizing* the income statement that the prospective seller submits.

Often, there are one-time-only expenses or revenue components that will not be a regular part of the business in the future. The normalization of the income statement via the pro forma modeling is required to "purify" the financial performance so the buyer and seller have a firm grasp on the post-transaction of earnings potential. Other adjustments may include one-time-only expenses and/or some semi-business (i.e., semi-personal) costs that should not be considered in the normalized pro forma income statement.

Additionally, the prospective seller is justified in considering futuristic trends for increased revenue attributable to the post-transaction operating structure. While these should be carefully crafted and not over- or understated, the final normalized income statement is an essential component of the valuation and/or QofE undertaking. With this backdrop, let's consider in greater detail these essential financial analyses, beginning with the valuation process and then the much more utilized QofE analysis.

VALUATION PROCESSES

In the past, when health systems purchased practices, their independent appraiser/valuator completed a formal valuation review. A valuation process, which is more of an appraisal of the practice or healthcare entity, applies one of three methodologies or approaches. The income approach, by far the most acceptable approach to valuation, uses a discounted flow methodology. Market and cost approaches may have applicability yet are not as commonplace as the income approach.

Most PE transactions do not include a valuation process, but it is a possibility within the context of the overall financial review of a prospective buyer and is completed by an independent valuation/QofE expert. Thus, the valuation process is not prominently applied for PE transactions, whereas it is applied for health system, practice, or related healthcare entity transactions.

Nonetheless, we have included an example of a simplistic approach to valuation that might be used to assign and conclude the value of the business

		Normalized FYE 2023	Y1	Y2	Projected Y3	Y4	Y5	Terminal Year
Total Revenue		$1,000,000	$1,050,000	$1,076,000	$1,098,000	$1,120,000	$1,142,000	$1,185,000
EBITDA		$225,000	$236,000	$242,000	$247,000	$252,000	$257,000	$262,000
Depreciation and Amortization		($50,000)	($50,000)	($50,000)	($50,000)	($50,000)	($50,000)	($50,000)
Operating Profit (EBIT)		$175,000	$186,000	$192,000	$197,000	$202,000	$207,000	$212,000
Income Tax	28.00%		($52,080)	($53,760)	($55,160)	($56,560)	($57,960)	($59,360)
Net Operating Profit After Tax (NOPAT)			$133,920	$138,240	$141,840	$145,440	$149,040	$152,640
+ Non-Cash Expenses			$50,000	$50,000	$50,000	$50,000	$50,000	$50,000
+/- Decreases/(Increases) to Net Working Capital	12.00%		($6,000)	($3,120)	($2,640)	($2,640)	($2,640)	($2,760)
- Capital Expenditures			($50,000)	($50,000)	($50,000)	($50,000)	($50,000)	($50,000)
Free Cash Flow to the Firm			$127,920	$135,120	$139,200	$142,800	$146,400	$149,880
Terminal Value								$1,152,923
Weighted Average Cost of Capital	15.00%							
Present Value Factor			0.93	0.81	0.71	0.61	0.53	0.53
Present Value of Free Cash Flow			$119,286	$109,565	$98,151	$87,556	$78,055	$614,696

Fair Market Value of Invested Capital	$1,107,309
Minus: Interest-bearing Liabilities	($100,000)
Fair Market Value of Equity (100%)	$1,007,309

FIGURE 4.1: Discounted Cash Flow

Acquisition by PE Firm		
Practice Revenue		$50,000,000
Total Physician Compensation (Pre-Haircut)		$25,000,000
Total Number of Physicians		10
Haircut (10% x $25,000,000)	10%	$2,500,000
Reduced Comp per Physician		$250,000
Multiple on Haircut		9
Transaction Value (9 x $2,500,000)		$22,500,000
Proceeds of Transaction per Physician ($22,500,000÷10)		$2,250,000

FIGURE 4.2: PE Multiple of Earnings Approach[1]

that is being acquired (see Figure 4.1). This model uses the income approach and includes the income scrape or haircut of compensation as a permanent reduction applied throughout the post-transaction relationship. The PE investor requires such a conclusion to allow for an adequate return on their investment over a brief time. Another transaction or liquidity event will follow, often referred to as the "second bite of the apple." Some of the sales proceeds will be rolled over and reinvested in the "Newco" equity.

In addition, in Figure 4.2, we have evaluated the discounted cash flow (DCF) calculation of Figure 4.1 utilizing the market approach. This simplistic example illustrates how an earnings before interest, taxes, depreciation, and amortization (EBITDA) conclusion is derived via the income scrape and a market multiple applied to that EBITDA to derive value.

OVERVIEW OF QofE

The valuation process utilizing an income or market approach is not as significant in determining a sales price within a PE-backed entity transaction as is the utilization of QofE analysis. Therefore, we will focus more on the QofE process than the valuation efforts.

The goal is to derive enterprise value for the business being considered within the overall sale. This emphasis allows for a "deep dive" financial analysis of what the QofE entails. The QofE encompasses not only the normalization process outlined above but also a series of futuristic assumptions relevant to the prospective purchase. These projections are not "pie-in-the-sky" calculations; they are based on efforts that are both relevant and probable. Thus, it is essential for an independent QofE expert to review these entries seriously, from normalization adjustment to futuristic assumptions that affect the concluded EBITDA.

The QofE analysis is a specific process performed by an independent expert, often a financial consultant or valuation firm with specific expertise in healthcare transactions. This analysis may also be performed by an accounting firm with similar subspecialized expertise. The firm completing the QofE should have expertise in the nuances of physician practices and related healthcare entities.

Typically, the QofE process begins with historical financial statements followed by application of the normalization process. Here, the existing income statement is altered based on the adjustments to revenues and expenses that the business will incur —either personal, semi-personal, or non-existent going forward. All adjustments toward normalization will determine the final restated or normalized income statement.

From there, futuristic assumptions and other relevant and expected realistic or reasonable growth and/or expense adjustments are applied to determine the subsequent years' pro forma financial performance. While some of the value and the derived EBITDA will be a result of the normalization plus futuristic assumptions processes, the QofE firm must independently conclude as to the viability and veracity of the EBITDA totals as derived. As EBITDA is the key derivative of the QofE process, it warrants additional explanation below.

A QofE will consider appropriate market multiples of EBITDA to derive the initial valuation or QofE conclusions. Thus, the QofE process is a thorough, intensive review of historical performance and, even more, it is the realistic reflection of future performance post-transaction. While this is similar to the valuation/appraisal process, it is much more of a prospective review than a historical one, whereas the valuation process encompasses much of the latter.

Some would call the QofE a financial due diligence process. It does entail this level of analysis in that it is an intensive review of the healthcare entity being considered within a PE transaction and more specifically, its historical but equally as important expected economic performance in the future.

The derivation of the QofE's conclusions is centered around the definition of EBITDA. Because EBITDA is made "pure" to exclude non-cash expenses such as amortization and depreciation but is also considered extraneous to actual performance components of interest and taxes, it has become the metric widely considered the most relevant indicator for concluding the enterprise value of that business.

Technically, EBITDA is not a GAAP (Generally Accepted Accounting Principles) metric and would not be considered within the actual financial statements as reported to a bank or the public or other entity, nor would it necessarily be the subject of an audit opinion. However, for measurement of a PE-related transaction, it is by far the best indicator.

The reason it is an effective indicator is that it measures the healthcare business under consideration and its ability to generate working capital/cash flow and removes the effects of certain capital structures and business conditions such as interest and taxes that may not apply in the same manner to the post-transaction purchaser.

Usually, purchasers will engage in a buy-side QofE analysis before they submit a firm offer to the prospective seller. Likewise, sellers will engage an independent firm to perform a sell-side QofE analysis. Either party may then consider their independent QofE conclusions and reconcile between the two. Within the process, there should be a convergence of conclusions that results in the agreed-upon EBITDA upon which the purchase/sales price is based.

After the EBITDA is derived through the QofE process, a multiple of that total is applied and is the ultimate derivation of the purchase price.

Key Benefits

QofE satisfies many other means-to-an-end requirements within the entire process. Therefore, a QofE has both direct and indirect value relative to the overall transaction process.

The key benefits of the QofE are:

- *Accurate depiction of historical performance.* The QofE analysis performed by an expert serves as an independent validation of the veracity of historical financial statements. Often, these financial statements of a healthcare entity such as a medical practice are not fully based upon GAAP and may entail some expenses that should be "normalized." QofE analyzers should be experienced to the degree that they discern and adjust for certain expenses that are not fully applicable to the healthcare entity under consideration.

  For example, many medical practices include certain expenses for extraneous, albeit quasi-business purposes, running through their practice and thus as a part of their income statement. While we do not debate the veracity of such procedures, these expenses are often within that entity's financial statement. To normalize is to reflect and adjust (up or down) for costs that are not directly relevant to the practice. More often, these expenses are costs that will not be present post-transaction. Therefore, they need to be removed within the normalization process.

  Revenue may also be normalized in that the post-transaction relationship could include revenue that a medical practice or more specifically a physician generates outside of the practice but after a PE transaction is completed, would be included. Therefore, in normalizing revenue, those amounts should be added to what would be the post-transaction totals.

- *Adjustments for compensation.* Ideally, the normalization should include some income scrape to the physician's compensation to derive an earnings amount (EBITDA) upon which the value will be placed.

- *Adjustments for other revenues and expenses.* In addition to the normalization process and those adjustments considered within it, there may be non-recurring or out-of-period revenues and expenses to be adjusted. Perhaps there are costs that are not run through the practice or healthcare entity that need to be considered within the QofE-based income statement.
- *Accounting methodologies.* Many medical practices are still accounted for on a cash basis. While this may be acceptable within PE transactions, the more accurate accounting standard is an accrual basis that is as close to GAAP as possible. Adjustments for non-cash items to derive EBITDA can still be made as the restated income statement is completed.
- *Standardization.* The QofE is not only accepted but in many cases expected to be completed. At times, only a buy-side QofE will be completed, but the seller benefits greatly from a sell-side QofE, which will give the seller an independently derived and validated EBITDA total, which can be used to negotiate the transaction purchase price with more accuracy.
- *A working capital threshold.* Working capital is an integral part of the go-forward nature of the business post-transaction. As such, the QofE usually considers working capital on a month-to-month basis, deriving some degree of accuracy of what that total would be within any given period. The analysis should consider accounts receivable, especially those amounts that are questionable as to collectability. Other items to be considered include inventory that is not sellable or usable in any way. Therefore, developing a standard for working capital is a significant by-product of the QofE analysis.
- *Negotiating foundation.* As we alluded to above, the QofE is the standard performed by independent experts, which will further both the seller and the buyer's ability to "reach a deal" more quickly with confidence that the numbers are accurate and validated. While the QofE entails an additional cost to both the buyer and seller (assuming each party has a QofE completed), in many ways it will save money because it expedites the negotiation and ultimate economic terms processes of the transaction.

QofE Report Example

There is no right or wrong way to standardize a reporting process for such a formal document; however, certain components of the QofE are essential within the formal reporting process.

While there will be nuances to each individual analysis, an example of the general formatting for the QofE is presented in Appendix E, which, in our view, is most applicable. The report is redacted so no numbers are included; however, we have left applicable notes along with certain conclusions and recommendations as they would have applied to the actual report.

Following the proper formatting of reporting is essential in that the report is intended to be a standardization of all such QofE analyses that a given expert would provide. Moreover, the report should reflect the expectations of the party engaging the QofE expert to complete this analysis. Finally, it is important for the report to be easy to understand in the context of non-financial experts who would utilize it to negotiate and agree to a sale or purchase price.

Appendix E presents a cover letter and other exhibits that explain to the client the QofE process and some of its related boundaries for completion, such as the fact that it does not constitute an audit or a review of financial statements per se. The cover letter provides a summary of those boundaries.

In addition, the report comprises various exhibits that the reader should consider in reviewing its findings. Overall terms and limitations are typically documented, followed by summarization including adjustments, footnotes, and an adjusted income statement. Following those sections are sections and related exhibits for due diligence adjustments, pro forma adjustments, and quality of revenue in general.

Finally, the report would include the normalization of the reconciliation and cash flow analysis, along with some presentation of historical financial statements. The typical QofE report provides compelling information for facilitating the transaction from both the buyer's and the seller's standpoint.

KEY STEPS

Performing a QofE analysis requires a range of professional skills and industry expertise. We recommend that a QofE be performed only by an independent expert who typically works in related transactional matters pertaining to healthcare entities. Otherwise, the QofE experts' ability to best derive QofE conclusions for a healthcare entity would be suspect. The nuances of the healthcare industry should be understood.

In completing the typical QofE process, the following six steps and considerations are typically characteristic of the analysis for a healthcare entity.

1. *Data Needs.* Accurate and complete data are essential, both historically and prospectively. These data must be as reasonably accurate although audited financial statements are not required if the information is deemed to be accurately summarized.

2. *Management Interview.* Speaking with the management and or owners of the healthcare entity is essential. The interview should include asking questions relative to the nuances of their business, how it is operated, and specific things especially important to the healthcare entity, particularly the medical practice (such as physician compensation and the physician scrape). These matters are imperatively required and best determined through the management interview.

3. *Quality of Revenue.* Revenue within the healthcare entity can be nebulous at times, even to the point of being uncertain. If, for example, accounting is based on an accrual basis, there should always be an adjustment from accrual to cash that reflects the actual dollars received as opposed to the revenue accrued and anticipated to be received. The discounted fees are a reason for this in that the fees (and thus revenue) may not always be as accurate as those received after the discounting process occurs.

4. *Due Diligence and Pro Forma Adjustments.* The normalization of the financial statements is important, even essential. Due diligence will reflect on the determination of any specific adjustments that work toward normalization of the income statement. The QofE valuator's understanding of this process is imperative.

5. *Healthcare-specific Considerations.* The independent QofE analyst must also understand the nuances of healthcare, how physician compensation works, the concept of discounting fees, regulatory requirements, and myriad other issues that are reflected in the financial reporting process.

6. *Balance Sheet Considerations and Working Capital.* The importance of working capital to the overall QofE analysis must be accurately

depicted as the transaction is completed. Often, this balance is higher than expected but does not become definitive until later in the transaction structuring. It should be a by-product of the QofE analysis and thus a targeted amount that the seller agrees to remain in the business for the buyer.

While balance sheet considerations might not seem to be as important to the QofE process, if there are certain things that are "parked" there, they may affect the income statement as finalized within the QofE analysis. The savvy QofE analyst should be cognizant of such possibilities and thoroughly review the balance sheet.

SUMMARY

In summary, the QofE analysis and overall valuation process is one of the most important, if not essential, in the continuum of a healthcare/PE-backed entity transaction. Without a QofE, it is difficult for the buyer or the seller to be certain that the targeted price is accurate, timely, fair, and reasonable (to both sides).

While there may be instances where a QofE can either be abridged or not completed to enable the completion of a validated transaction, it is becoming rare. The QofE, when done properly, is the standard that establishes the watermark of value to complete the transaction fairly.

REFERENCE

1. Reiboldt M, Welch B. Pursuing the Private Equity Model for Physician Practice Transactions. Coker. 2022. Accessed June 11, 2024. https://assets-global.website-files.com/6596e79ed39ae84161e4c191/65f08e5e54e0f5b541ed13c0_Pursuing%20the%20Private%20Equity%20Model%20for%20Physician%20Practice%20Transactions.pdf.

CHAPTER 5

Physician Dynamics in Private Equity Transactions

MOST PHYSICIANS ARE AWARE of private equity partnerships and understand them quite well; others are eager to learn more. As physicians' knowledge of the economic and non-economic aspects of private equity (PE) arrangements grows, mindsets and perspectives relative to PE affiliation vary. Some physicians take a negative view of private equity affiliation, some take a positive view, and most are somewhere between.

Among the many private equity-backed companies, most are specialized within a limited boundary of disciplines. All have similar features, but a variation in structures and outcomes requires physicians to understand those variations to clear misconceptions and acknowledge their limitations. Helping physicians understand these variations is imperative, as many misconceptions exist. In this chapter, we go inside the heads of physicians for insight into their perspectives on private equity affiliation.

PHYSICIAN OPTIONS RELATIVE TO PRACTICE STRUCTURE

Private equity's entry into the healthcare industry, especially over the past couple of decades, has changed the paradigm for physicians and their options for practice structure. A discussion of private equity and physicians' perspectives begins with a broad definition of the basic employment options, professional services, and other affiliation scenarios. The following are the options:

1. *Remaining fully private within a physician group*, merging with other private practices.
2. *Hospital affiliation*, either through direct employment or a professional services agreement (PSA).
3. *Private equity partnering*

4. *Hybrid models* based on all or some of the above structures.

Physicians who have a choice in how they structure their medical practice may change that structure over the course of their career. Rarely would a physician affiliate with a private equity-backed firm when just starting in practice; however, he or she may join a group that is already affiliated with private equity.

Often physicians who start in private practice eventually evolve to hospital/health system affiliation, usually within the employment framework, and sometimes through a physician service agreement (PSA). Increasingly, groups with PSAs employ hybrid models that are typically carve-outs of specific practice elements accompanied by a private equity-backed affiliation. A vital component of these innovative structures must be total compliance with regulatory requirements and structures, both economic and otherwise.

It is almost inevitable that physicians in private practice will eventually arrive at a major crossroads in their career path. The first choice is hospital or health system employment or a professional service agreement (PSA); the second is a private equity affiliation. Another possible route is a hybrid structure between a hospital/health system and private equity affiliation.

The physicians' mindset, their perspectives on their careers, how they practice, and the potential financial ramifications of all these conditions are imperative to consider and select. As noted in various scenarios, none of these options is right or wrong.

The decision with whom to partner should be based on the physician's education, research, and overall comfort level, with no full acceptance or rejection of any model. Each of these four options or any variable has a history of successes and failures. *None of these models or variables is a totally right or wrong choice, including private equity affiliation.*

What key points should physicians consider when ultimately deciding how best to structure their practice? Some merely allow their group or network colleagues to make the decision, opting to "go with the crowd." Although this decision may be best for "the crowd," it may not be the best choice for long-term sustainability; therefore, it is critical that physicians understand the private equity model, the hospital employment and/or PSA model, and the range of variables in between. Again, the decision for any model is not black and white; it is gray.

How does a physician or related group decide whether to affiliate or opt to remain fully independent and private? Does it matter where that physician is in his or her career path (age, years to practice, etc.)? What structure provides the most (or least) security? What specialties work best for private equity affiliation?

What about quality and clinical freedom to practice medicine based on the structure, whether it is private equity, hospital affiliation, or private independent practice? Is private equity only for the older physicians' (i.e., 10 years or less remaining to practice) career situation? These questions deserve serious thought and answers.

We will explore these issues later in this chapter, keeping in mind that the answers may differ, depending on individual situations.

PHYSICIANS AND PRIVATE EQUITY OPPORTUNITIES

As stated earlier, the history of private equity affiliation with physicians is brief. The vast capital resources within private equity-backed firms have generated opportunities for early adopters and those who are currently considering or completing private equity affiliations.

As in their association with health systems and hospitals, physicians have experienced both negative and positive results in their affiliations with private equity. Private equity, as it deployed the resources through its management services organizations (MSOs) and other related operational entities, has effected efficient practice management more successfully than many health systems that demonstrated inferior performance when they tried to manage and operate physician practices.

While many health systems are managing physician practices better, others fall short operationally; however, overall, private equity and health systems have progressed in their relationships, management, and partnerships with physician groups. Healthcare patients, while continuing to vocalize their concerns about the current delivery system, have been on the sidelines regarding whether a physician group should be affiliated with private equity or a health system or remain private.

Private equity firms that have invested and injected capital into practices and other healthcare service entities are credited with improving the overall patient experience. True, private equity firms have a definitive for-profit motivation and mission, but all hospitals and health systems, even those that are technically not-for-profit, must also realize margins to make ends meet.

The benefits for physicians who affiliate with private equity are numerous and may be fiscally and relationally compelling, but those affiliations are not without their challenges. Physicians seeking to avoid administrative hassles have looked to health systems and hospitals for assistance; being employed while allowing the hospitals to assume the management role, however, has yielded only mediocre to inferior results.

Nonetheless, regulatory pressures, new payment models, and generally lower reimbursement rates from payers have continued to create challenges and stresses for physicians, including those who affiliate with private equity. However, private equity's for-profit motivation tends to make it more efficient than hospitals and health systems, though the latter are progressively improving their performance.

Physicians want to practice medicine and provide their patients with high-quality treatment; they also want to receive remuneration commensurate to their risks, training, and position in society. Selling a practice to private equity and taking employment can allow physicians to realize these goals and objectives without the burden of administrative hassles.

For younger physicians, *quality of life* may be a reason to go with private equity in spite of the disadvantages of income scrape, income repair, and rollover investment. However, since private equity rolls up many physician practices into a larger platform entity, the smaller practice gains the benefits of being in a larger group while still practicing as an individual. Cost savings can result in a greater ability to negotiate reimbursement rates with payers, particularly commercial ones, and the opportunity to take on value-based payment structures.

Physicians have many reasons to consider partnering with private equity not only to reduce the administrative workload but also to create a scalable entity with considerable market prowess that boosts their compensation and gives them an equity stake and a future "second bite of the apple."

Hospitals and health systems can provide some advantages, but they have fallen short in management and structure. Hospitals and health systems looking at long-term opportunities have wisely partnered in three-way transactions with private equity; here, PE often provides the management's support that hospitals have been lacking. Being willing to "split the pie" three ways is a challenge for many health systems, even a non-starter with no chance of success, but it is a negotiation option that physicians (and hospitals) should consider and embrace.

RELEVANT MATTERS FOR PHYSICIANS

We previously posed several questions physicians typically ask as they consider private equity affiliation. Although the list is not all-inclusive, it covers the landscape of physicians' concerns, depending on their understanding of how private equity functions. Following are questions for discussion.

What relevant matters should physicians consider when deciding how and where best to affiliate, or even whether to affiliate, opting to remain independent and private?

While economics is near the top of the list, it is likely not the most relevant factor. With economics claiming the top spot, financial ramifications are a "close second" in the list of relevant matters.

The first and most important concern for physicians is how they can function as healthcare providers; they must be assured that the structure will support them, and they must know that the structure will be adequate to address their clinical needs and preferences. Other pertinent matters include the management and governance structure, the provision for making independent decisions (especially clinical ones), and the relationship that will result after the transaction.

Physicians, especially those who are not savvy or interested in structural relationships (i.e., who does or does not employ them), often feel they are being "bounced around" with different models and structures. They are concerned about their practice of medicine and serving their patients well.

Private equity can operate within this structure, allowing all these needs and preferences to prevail. Although some individuals believe that private equity is "just about the money," we disagree. Private equity investors clearly want to align with high-quality providers and supply the infrastructure and support systems to ensure quality results; overall, private equity is concerned with maintaining high-quality healthcare.

Eventually, even with a for-profit business goal in place (and in total compliance with regulatory requirements), practicing with proper clinical protocols and assurances will inherently enhance the value of the business, along with supporting the physicians' need for clinical excellence.

What are the key questions physicians should ask?

In the context of the private equity deal and structure, the key questions to address include issues discussed above, including the economic and financial terms and conditions, and the structure of the economics of private equity deals, which include an understanding of the income scrape, income repair, rollover equity, and other specific facets to typical private equity deals. It is imperative to address and understand these matters.

Other questions to be answered concern elements of governance and leadership, long-term play, and the "second bite of the apple," including recapitalization, which will likely occur in the future. Issues such as succession planning and funds to be paid at retirement, non-competes, and restrictive covenants, should be a part of the dialogue, and clarification should be provided to physicians who are considering affiliation with private equity. (See Appendix B for more details and checklists of areas to consider, along with due diligence requirements in private equity transactions.)

Can any specific option provide the most comfort for a physician?

Understanding the private equity model, the employment model of hospitals, professional services agreements, etc., is imperative for the physician who can then analyze what makes the most sense, based on their comfort level and other criteria. Relying on other physicians' judgment is not appropriate. Each physician should attempt to discern the process, whether it's private equity, hospital employment, remaining private, merging into a private group, etc.

Does it matter where the physician is in his or her career path?

Yes, it makes an enormous difference. Older physicians are typically more receptive to private equity transactions and working relationships because they are nearer to their retirement. A succession plan, which usually entails up-front money that they would not otherwise receive, is a factor that influences his or her leaning toward completing private equity affiliation.

Younger physicians find it more difficult to see the benefits of private equity affiliation; the income scrape alone, with no assurances of complete income repair, is an inhibitor to younger physicians who have at least 10 to 20 years left to practice.

Does this mean that younger physicians will not do private equity deals? Of course not. Even younger physicians may agree to proceed with private equity; the same option applies to hospital employment or PSAs. With pros and cons to all models, none is perfect, but where a physician is in his or her career influences his view of private equity affiliation.

What are the risks of going in a particular direction and then realizing it was not a good decision?

The risks exist, but an error is unlikely if the right questions are asked and answered on the front side. Moreover, there are always opportunities to stop private equity or any other affiliation deal before consummation.

If the "red flags" appear early on or even later in the process, they should not be overlooked. Physicians should draw concerns to the attention of their advisers and decide at that time whether to proceed. There should always be a point in the deal at which a physician and his or her colleagues deem it best not to proceed and the process is brought to an end.

What structure provides the most (or least) security?

This is a difficult question to answer because any of these structures, whether hospital affiliation, private practice in an independent setting, or aligned with private equity, have risks relative to security. Just as there is no perfect model, there is no model that ensures long-term security. Longer-term contracts, fewer non-compete restrictions, and legal economic gain all promote greater assurance of security.

What specialties work best for private equity affiliation? What specialties are typically more questionable as to their success within private equity structures?

Most private equity deals in the past were with physician specialists who were not of great interest to hospitals and health systems for employment. Dermatology, pathology, radiology, anesthesiology, and other hospital-based specialties are of great interest to hospitals but are not typically structured under employment models. Moreover, PSAs usually continue to function, even when the practice specialty is aligned with private equity.

Over time, some more traditional clinic-based specialties have surfaced and are attractive to private equity firms. These include orthopedics, neurosurgery, pain management and other musculoskeletal specialties, gastroenterology, urology, and cardiology. Primary care, however, may be of interest to private equity if the group is large enough, has a sufficient critical mass of providers, and is already involved in shared savings and value-based reimbursement programs.

What about quality and clinical freedom to practice medicine based on the structure, whether it is private equity, hospital affiliation, or private independent practice?

We believe clinical freedom and quality are the primary goals and objectives of all these touchpoints of affiliation. A physician can establish a practice to satisfy his or her professional goals and objectives no matter the type or source of affiliation, including private equity.

What will potentially stand the test of time for a physician regardless of the stage of their career?

The success to be found in completing a private equity deal will, over time, prove the decision to have been right or wrong. Its appraisal will vary, based on the structure and its tangible and intangible components.

Is private equity only for older physicians (i.e., those with 10 years or less remaining to practice)?

No, private equity can work well for physicians at all levels and stages of their careers. While older physicians are more interested in private equity for obvious reasons, deals can be struck to accommodate younger physicians, as discussed in other chapters.

SUMMARY

There you have it! Basic questions asked and answered. There are many things to consider, with the only absolute being structuring within proper compliance boundaries. Sorting through the terms, structures, expectations, goals, and myriad other areas of consideration can be daunting, especially for non-business-trained physicians.

The best decision-making for determining the course of action comes through education on private equity and other affiliation options; engaging competent and unbiased advisors and legal counsel is essential.

This chapter is not intended to advocate for or against a practice affiliation decision, either with PE or another model; its goal is to inform of what is included in any course of action.

CHAPTER 6

Economic Pros and Cons in Private Equity Transactions

A S WE EXPLORE IN GREATER DETAIL the pros and cons of private equity transactions, primarily focused on physician groups and related services, it is essential to consider the economic advantages and disadvantages. There are both positives and negatives related to economic structures, depending in large part on the individual physician's personal and career goals and aspirations. Those physicians who are in the latter years of their careers will find the economics of PE transactions more acceptable, if not preferred.

Many private groups struggle to have in place a retirement plan that provides little more than a payment for the tangible assets and accounts receivable physicians leave behind. This results in small distributions at retirement. Private equity, on the other hand provides more economic opportunity (with caveats as we explore in this chapter).

The economics must work for all members of the group, not just the older ones. Accordingly, all PE/medical practice transactions must offer balance, if not some middle ground, which allows the entire group to pursue and complete the PE affiliation.

ECONOMIC COMPONENTS

Most PE transactions involving physician groups include similar economic structures. Physicians should include not only the basic criteria, but also the financial modeling as a fundamental part of the evaluation process.

The private equity purchaser often supplies a letter, often called the indication of interest (IOI). This is a simple, one- to two-page letter that reflects the initial financial analysis of the potential purchaser and outlines the key components based on the initial evaluation of the offer.

Assuming it evokes sufficient interest, further analysis may result in a more formal (but still non-legally binding) letter of intent (LOI). The LOI drills down even more into economic terms and conditions and usually requests exclusivity for a time. During that exclusivity period, the purchaser performs much more due diligence, which lends even more specificity to the economic terms. During the due diligence post-LOI period, non-economic terms are also pursued.

To explore the key economic components in more detail, we dissect them by major components, rounding out the typical overall economic terms and conditions.

Upfront Funds

Most private medical practices do not generate earnings that are left undistributed. Retained earnings are a rare characteristic of private practices. Therefore, when we consider *book value*, it is usually just the net book value of the depreciable assets on the balance sheet. Accounts receivable could be included but usually are not directly purchased and a part of the working capital adjustment at closing.

One of the distinguishing traits of private equity transactions is that significant dollars typically are paid upfront to the partners of the practice. In the typical PE deal, these upfront funds are created through a restatement of earnings before income taxes, depreciation, and amortization (EBITDA). This means that a combination of some expense reductions for quasi-personal expenses that are run through the practice are added to the bottom line. But mostly, EBITDA is created through the *income scrape* or *haircut* process. The income scrape is a reduction of physician (essential partners only) compensation. This could be as much as 20%–30% of the most recent and analytically modeled compensation for the partner physicians.

For example, if a partner physician is making $1 million per year in total cash compensation, which typically would include a distribution of all earnings for a given year, that amount is reduced in the PE modeling to $800,000. The $200,000 difference is moved to EBITDA. If there are five partners in the practice and each has similar scenarios, then $1 million of EBITDA (5 x $200,000) is created through the income scrape. That EBITDA is applied to a competitively priced multiple to generate the "value" for the practice.

In our example, if we have $1 million of EBITDA and the multiple is market-based at 10, the value is $10 million. Typically, this would include the tangible assets being inherently included within the offer total, although there could be a scenario in which those assets are valued in addition to the EBITDA multiple.

Payment at closing is therefore more attractive to older physicians who would otherwise not realize such a value upon retirement. Moreover, the older physicians are usually at a point in their lives and careers wherein they can take the income scrape or reduction in compensation post-transaction. That income scrape or reduction in compensation is then implemented by the PE purchaser post-transaction.

The post-transaction compensation is often a significant negative for the physician partners, especially those who have many years remaining to practice. The income scrape is real, and a reduction in pay post-transaction is likewise.

Notwithstanding these realities, there can be opportunities for *income repair* post-transaction. By this, we mean that the PE acquirer works alongside the practice to identify genuine opportunities for increasing the bottom line post-transaction. Part of that increased bottom line could be shared with the physicians via additional compensation returning to them.

An example of income repair is payer contracting and reimbursement structures. If, for example, the private equity firm can negotiate better commercial payer rates, those improved rates could be shared with the physicians in the form of their post-transaction compensation. Such would offset the otherwise quantified income scrape, thus resulting in some remediation of that lost income.

The timeline for complete income repair (i.e., returning the physicians to their pre-transaction compensation) can be a lengthy period. This should be analyzed prior to finalizing the practice sale.

Another feature is *rollover equity*. Rollover equity is typically manifested by the practice selling 100% of its equity to the private equity sponsor. In turn, a percentage, usually 20%–30% of that sale, is reinvested in a new entity ("Newco.") That Newco is not only the remnant of the practice, but typically includes other similar practices as aggregated within either the platform of the purchased practice or some other consortium of previous PE-sponsored purchases; thus, these form that platform.

While the rollover equity results in fewer upfront payments at closing, it provides the incentive to remain interested and focused on the success of the Newco. However, when the Newco is sold as part of a *recapitalization process,* a second return on invested funds results. It is during that recapitalization process that the private equity sponsor would typically exit and sell their interest, which also includes the minority interest (i.e., the rollover equity) among the physician practice partners who originally sold the practice to the PE entity.

Therefore, rollover equity could result in a significant "second bite of the apple," meaning that the investment of 20%–30% could render another significant multiple of an even greater EBITDA, given the fact that it would not be just the original practice but others that have since been purchased and aggregated within that platform. Thus, because there would be much more sold within the recapitalization (due to acquisitions that the private equity sponsor would complete prior to the recapitalization), the "second bite of the apple" may result in as much or more proceeds than the first component sale. Hence, greater value.

These economic features are in play but are with risks. Like any investment, the rollover equity has no guaranteed assurances of return, although depending on the situation, there could be some guaranteed return and/or earnings distributions that go to the rollover equity investor physicians. While these are not common, they depend on the entry level (i.e., whether the practice is the platform entity) plus other areas of consideration.

Such factors as earnings (at least those to supply enough to pay the income taxes passed through, plus a possible guaranteed return paid at recapitalization) would improve the economic considerations assessing the PE transaction.

These basic economic realities and other features we explore below and consider in greater detail are essential for the physician/sell-side to understand. There are risks and benefits in each of these economic components.

PE MODEL VALUATION

How does the valuation process work in the typical PE model? We start with deriving EBITDA and then applying a *market multiple*. This is a simple approach toward valuation and does not include what has historically been a more acceptable *income approach* utilizing a *discounted cash flow methodology* for the valuation of a medical practice. Such an approach has often been the methodology of hospitals, valuing medical practices for acquisition. For

PE firms, however, , *the market approach* is most acceptable and typically a result of the restatement of earnings to derive EBITDA through the income scrape or haircut process described earlier in this chapter. Therefore, the typical steps for PE valuation include the following:

1. Determine the income scrape/haircut. The haircut (i.e., compensation reduction, also referred to as the "compensation scrape") is applied across all physicians/partners but may vary by provider.
2. Develop a pro forma financial model. The haircut is turned into EBITDA with growth over a five-year projection period (Note: There are important and detailed steps that must go into the development of these models, but for this discussion, we assume the model follows all relevant and appropriate standards.)
3. For PE transactions, the market approach utilizing multiples of EBITDA is most common in actual applications.

In these simplified examples, we illustrate the typical valuation process. The income scrape is an important component in that this reduction of compensation while creating the earnings which in turn contribute to the upfront value (usually less the rollover equity, as reinvested), is somewhat arbitrary.

This income has been artificially created; however, the compensation reduction in the post-transaction working relationship is very real. While it could vary between the physician partners within the practice, it is still a compensation reduction post-transaction. The income repair is important as the private equity firm is looking for ways to mitigate the physicians' loss of income to keep them engaged and focused.

PRACTICE AGREEMENTS REGARDING VALUATION AND UPFRONT DOLLARS

The private equity firm is most concerned about the overall EBITDA derivation, the multiple, and thus, the calculation of the upfront payment to the practice. Within the practice, however, and depending on its legal structure, there may be varying amounts of income scrape per physician and, in turn, differing amounts reinvested in the rollover equity.

This can be an accommodation to the younger physicians, for example, who are not enamored with private equity transactions and working relationships. The PE sponsors want all physicians to be focused and engaged and they believe that some investment in rollover equity is essential. As for the distribution of the upfront payment, again this could vary by physician status, although the easier way to implement this is by requiring each physician an equal amount of income scrape and rollover equity reinvested.

ROLLOVER EQUITY CONSIDERATIONS

We have discussed rollover equity and explained its derivation. Now, we will discuss the theories behind the rollover equity, which hopefully are positive for the entire transaction.

Rollover equity is a new investment that ideally is a result of an aggregation of not just the initial platform practice, but several others that are acquired by the PE sponsor and aggregated into the "Newco." As to whether this is a wise investment, only time will tell, but in concept, this aggregation creates a larger entity with greater value for attracting a new investor somewhere down the road.

Usually, the rollover equity is realized via a second return to those investors within three to seven years after the initial transaction. Typically, there are little, if any, monies distributed from the rollover investment on an ongoing basis. There could be some distributions relative to a pass-through of income/earnings subject to federal and state income taxes at the individual investor level; however, beyond that, the distributions will be minimal.

Since the physicians who sold their practice have invested in a minority interest in the rollover entity, they would have little say as to distributions or when the subsequent second sale would take place. There may be opportunities for a retiring physician to divest his or her interest in the rollover entity before the second sale. This would be subject to the discretion of the majority owner and this equity would be replenished by an incoming physician partner to the practice, replacing the retiring physician whose equity and the rollover entity are being liquidated.

As to the value of that equity, it is typically tied to a set calculation representative of EBITDA, with a discount applied for lack of marketability and control, along with the possibility of an independent party completing such an appraisal for the sole purpose of redeeming equity of the departing physician investor.

Conversely, the equity may remain, even after the physician retires or otherwise terminates from the practice, awaiting the second sale. The second sale is usually a result of a recapitalization process wherein the private equity sponsor sells and does not reinvest in the platform being sold. Thus, that "second bite of the apple" is for the benefit of the majority owner, with the trailing benefits accruing to the physician investors, who are in the minority.

Thus, there are both positives and negatives to the lack of control. The negatives are that the physician investors in the rollover entity have little say as to timing, amounts of sale, valuations, etc. On a more positive note, though, they are participants in the investment in the rollover equity which historically has provided a handsome return on that investment. Thus, that "second bite of the apple" is real and positive and certainly worth the wait to be effectuated.

Rollover investment is also an important part of the continued connection of physicians to their practice. In other words, while not a majority of their proceeds from the sale, this investment is significant in its structure and the amount of the investment for the physicians to stay focused on performance and growth of the practice aggregation. This, along with the incentives from income repair from their income scrape and a nice return somewhere down the road, aligns incentives and creates economic positives for the overall transaction.

On a negative note, though, we reiterate that rollover investment is a risk. There are no guarantees for a return of any sort beyond their initial investment. Some transactions are structured wherein the physicians invested in the rollover entity have a guaranteed (or at least partially guaranteed) return. This, of course, is a result of the negotiations during the initial transaction process. Usually, only the platform physician practice entity benefits here. Nonetheless, it can be a significant positive toward doing the transaction when a guaranteed return that has some level of preferential payback is in place.

MULTIPLES OF EARNINGS

A fundamental part of the valuation equation is the multiple. This can vary with the structure of the transaction, its timing, its industry, and overall socioeconomic and inflationary trends, as well as myriad other things.

The platform practice will receive the best and highest multiples; those practices that follow will not receive as high a multiple as that initial transaction entailed. Multiples are negotiable; however, they reflect the PE sponsors' pro forma financial analysis and estimated return on investment. This can vary with not only the type of practice (i.e., its specialty, its ancillaries, and other accompanying entities such as surgery centers, imaging centers, etc.) that would potentially enhance the EBITDA, which would, in turn, enhance the value and result in a higher multiple.

A negative of multiples is sometimes couched in the structure of the private equity firm that declines to purchase 100% of the practice. For example, in some structures, the PE firm will acquire only 80% of the practice, with the remaining 20% unavailable to sell to any other outside party. In effect, the multiple is reduced because the PE firm is purchasing only 80% of the income stream of the practice.

Be wary of these types of structures; while they may not be "deal killers," they are, in effect, reductions of multiples that are veiled within the overall multiple that is offered. For example, if a 10 multiple is offered but only 80% of the EBITDA is being acquired, that, in effect, is only an 8 multiple (80% x 10). True, the remaining 20% may be left for the physicians through income/earnings distributions, but this is not always 100% assured either. Thus, the transaction must be scrutinized by expert advisers who assist the practice throughout this entire process.

POST-TRANSACTION ECONOMICS

Physician compensation post-transaction is a direct result of the pre-transaction terms and conditions. Not only does this include the income scrape, but it also includes considerations for income repair, management services organization (MSO) structure, and other matters that relate to compensation. All are worthy of significant review and understanding. This also will affect the incoming physicians who are added to the practice via recruitment or other means post-transaction. Whether they should have guaranteed compensation in that they were not a part of the rollover or even the upfront paid at closing should be factored into the deal post-transaction.

Overall, compensation of the physicians and other providers post-transaction should be structured similarly to any other income distribution plan for a medical practice. While the income scrape will be in play for those participating investor physicians, it can be mitigated through negotiations with the PE firm. This should be done on the front side of the transaction, not after it is completed. Most practices will be allowed to have their own income distribution plan post-transaction some variability in how the monies are distributed, assuming the PE firm has agreed to the overall payment of the pools of money post-transaction.

All these factors should be clearly defined, understood, and negotiated before agreeing to the PE transaction. Modeling of the income distribution plan should be completed and, to the extent possible, should be "shadowed" against their existing plan. This illustrates to the physicians contemplating the PE transaction as to their income on a projected basis post-closing.

Income repair is a notable hot topic and is often touted by private equity firms as a significant part of their business and strategic plan that justifies the transaction. Income repair items can include better payer contracting of commercial rates, expanded ancillary services, reduced overhead due to efficient and aggregated centralized management, and overall areas that private equity firms, through their MSOs, believe will result favorably. Thorough due diligence and a critical eye toward these income repair items prior to the physicians agreeing to the PE transaction may lead to a level of assurance.

As a further matter and by way of example, if a prominent platform practice already has strong commercial payer contracting rates, that element of the income repair may not be as good. With reduced income repair opportunities, such becomes more realistic as a post-transaction negative, especially to those younger physicians who value their ability to earn greater compensation.

Likewise, private equity firms will often promote their ability through their MSOs by creating economies of scale cost savings and overall improved efficiencies in management. While this is a possibility, depending on where the practice lies within its current management and administrative efficiencies, these savings may not be as great.

SUMMARY

As we have considered the various terms and related processes, the economic pros and cons of PE transactions elicit many questions and required areas of scrutinization. Thus, an "eyes wide open" view of these economic pros and cons should prevail.

Those who are more positive toward private equity transactions may accentuate the positives and de-emphasize these negatives, but regardless of the position they take relative to the potential PE transaction, they should enlist appropriate levels of independent assistance to sort out and validate both the pluses and minuses. Otherwise, there is a high likelihood that at least some of the physicians will, post-transaction, lament the deal with disappointment and frustration, exclaiming that they did not know or understand the negatives that accompanied the positives of these transactions. Slowing down the process and ensuring that the economic pros and cons are considered, negotiated, and agreed on is essential.

CHAPTER 7

Non-Economic Pros and Cons of Private Equity

MUCH OF THE FOCUS AND ATTENTION in a private equity (PE) trans-action is on the financial or economic considerations involved with a given deal. Sellers want to know what a buyer is willing to pay for the enterprise they have built. Unsurprisingly, someone selling a business will want to understand the financial return they can expect. In the same way, a buyer or investor will have certain limitations in terms of the capital they can lay out, as well as the return they can expect to receive based on their respective investment models, deal structures, and hold timelines.

PE firms have institutional capital investors for whom they are obligated to return value; therefore, a solid PE investor is not likely to approach any transaction without a deep understanding of how they will ultimately extract value from every dollar they invest.

With that fact clearly understood, are the economic variables the only factors to consider when evaluating a transaction or seeking a capital partner? Is economic consideration critical? Certainly. Nevertheless, most people would agree that financial consideration is not the only crucial element in any sort of transaction, and this is certainly the case when talking about PE investments in healthcare services enterprises.

Unfortunately, the non-economic factors related to a transaction often end up having a much lower priority during a deal, and in many cases, we have seen them completely overlooked, resulting in issues that arise in the future that could have either been addressed and minimized earlier on, or even completely avoided.

ECONOMIC VS. NON-ECONOMIC CONSIDERATIONS

In previous chapters, we discussed many of the dynamics related to financial or economic considerations involved in PE deals. Valuation is the most obvious, referring to the value of the enterprise and how that value will translate into distributable proceeds for the seller. In addition, there are the return on investment (ROI) targets that a buyer might pursue compared to the capital outlay tied to that enterprise valuation. And, of course, one must look at the other financial-related factors we have discussed, such as provider compensation adjustments, tax treatment, retained equity, and many other elements associated with the economics of a particular transaction.

While each individual deal has its unique economic terms and financial structures, there generally are more straightforward considerations when it comes to a deal's economics.

The non-economic considerations are quite different. These are typically more subjective and lack clarity around what they are and how to address them with at least some degree of compromise and acceptable benefit for all parties involved. We often refer to these as "softer" issues in that the subjectivity associated with non-economic considerations typically requires more dynamic and flexible approaches in terms of how such factors can or should be addressed in an acceptable manner. Some non-economic factors are easier to address than others, but typically, this is the part of a deal where the ability to define and lay out perfectly how non-economic factors should be addressed can be challenging.

Some examples of common non-economic components of a deal are related to matters such as post-transaction governance, leadership plans, communications, branding, and decision-making. Each of these items can be broken down into many sub-sections, which typically evolve throughout the deal process and post-closing. Moreover, many of these matters are unique in terms of structure within each transaction.

For one deal, the plans around governance and leadership may be quite clear, whereas for another transaction, this may spark some controversy among the parties involved. In addition, this or some other non-economic factor might be a key point when a seller is evaluating potential buyers.

For instance, for a large group of physicians evaluating PE firms or platform companies to partner with, maintaining legacy leadership might be a priority or even a requirement to include in an agreement with a future partner. In such a case, when evaluating interested parties, this dialogue needs to take priority in any discussions, because if one potential seller has an existing model for their portfolio company's leadership that does not synchronize with the seller's needs, this will be a key factor in the decision-making process.

NON-ECONOMIC FACTORS

We were advising on a sales process where the client was a large surgical group down to the top three PE firms under consideration as a capital partner. In this case, each firm had an existing platform that our client would integrate upon the closing of the deal.

Across the three candidate firms, the financial offers, general deal structures, and other standard terms were mostly consistent. However, one of the platforms had recently gone through an exhaustive electronic health record (EHR) implementation project in which they had adopted and deployed a major information technology (IT) solution across all their providers and planned for all new additional groups to be integrated with this solution.

This integration requirement makes sense considering the firm's major investment in a solution and the challenges it had faced implementing it in a way that would be scalable for growth and create operational and financial synergies for future platform growth.

However, our client had also recently implemented a new IT solution across all providers and locations, which was a significant investment in money, time, and energy. Our client's leadership agreed they would not do that again anytime soon (or perhaps ever) because while the process had been a challenge, they too had partnered with a major vendor and had implemented the solution in a way that would be scalable into the future, thus reducing the chances of needing to change again anytime soon. What made this even more interesting is that the group's prior IT vendor was the same one the buyer candidate had partnered with, and the impetus behind the group changing to a new solution was based on how horrible an experience they had with their previous vendor.

Suffice it to say, the seller group did not view this positively, and they were not keen to not only change systems yet again but to return to a solution that was universally disliked among their providers and staff.

This factor was identified early, so it was not dropped in at the last minute. However, it remained a major negative throughout the evaluation process. There were discussions about our client remaining on their new system, even though the potential buyer had adopted their own IT system. The potential partner was not open to this idea, considering the previously stated factors related to integration synergies. Moreover, this recent IT investment was not something the potential buyer was willing to adjust in the valuation, whereas the other potential partners were more flexible in this regard, both agreed to leave the group on their newly implemented IT solution.

The less-than-flexible candidate firm was not immediately eliminated due to this red flag. They made it into the top three candidates. However, this was something the group's leadership and decision-makers repeatedly came back to.

To make this situation even more interesting, this buyer had offered the highest valuation by comparison, albeit the differences in financial consideration compared to the other two candidates were marginal. Still, the question was asked: Do we take a slightly higher valuation in return for having to go back to the IT platform they viewed so negatively (not to mention dealing with yet another changeover of IT solutions), or do we put greater emphasis on maintaining the stability they had achieved with their new technology platform in exchange for a slightly lower economic consideration?

When it came down to the final vote, the seller unanimously supported a lower valuation and maintained stability.

This is just one example that highlights how non-economic factors can make the difference between proceeding with a deal, backing out, or selecting one partner over others. The example not only emphasizes how non-economic considerations can influence decision-making and overall direction, but it also illustrates how identifying potential non-economic issues can significantly impact the potential future success of a partnership, however that success is measured.

If the group in this example had chosen to partner with a platform that offered more money, there would have been serious issues after the transaction when it came time to implement the IT solution across all their providers and locations. We have seen negative situations like this play out in many ways, but in this case, it could have led to negative responses from the many other providers who were not involved in the final decision, potentially causing some to leave the group, which would have negatively impacted the partnership going forward.

Not all non-economic factors related to a deal are as "cut and dry," however. Issues may arise that are much less objective. Occasionally, these are personality-related problems. For instance, if a buyer purchases a group that comes in with major changes that are (or perceived as) negatively restrictive for the seller, this can change personality dynamics, which in turn could reduce constructive interaction. Perhaps operational process changes are established, resulting in more work for staff and/or providers. This can negatively affect productivity and efficiency.

We have observed deals where proposed changes in leadership or leadership structures resulted in negative responses from the providers and staff, which again can create additional unforeseen negative effects down the road. Some buyers may bring certain regulatory requirements or related issues with them that need to be considered by a potential seller in terms of how such factors impact the way they have operated their business historically and what changes will be required in the future if they were to partner with that firm.

Governance, reporting, processes, staffing, and other factors that have little or nothing to do with valuation or financial models can all play significant roles in the future probability of success in a partnership. And it is safe to say that if any of these dynamics spill over into clinical services or management of how care is delivered in terms of provider/patient dynamics, this likely will not be received well by the providers to a point where achieving those longer-term financial returns are jeopardized.

SUMMARY

Overall, the potential non-economic considerations related to a deal with PE firms or PE-backed platforms are endless and varied. In many deals, no actual issues arise related to non-economic considerations; however, this does not mean there is nothing to consider regarding such factors. Just because there are no obvious issues does not mean that non-economic considerations do not exist. Such issues still need to be identified, addressed, and, if possible, agreed upon prior to a partnership being solidified.

IF there are issues, major or minor, these matters need to be addressed prior to a deal's closing, ideally with a solution agreed upon through compromises such that both the buyer and seller can benefit. This will not guarantee a long-term successful partnership (nothing will do that); however, it will go a long way toward ensuring future success and reducing pitfalls.

CHAPTER 8

Ancillaries and Private Equity Transactions

A NOTHER MAJOR CONSIDERATION in exploring the operational and strategic facets of healthcare private equity transactions is *ancillary services*. Ancillaries are any additional services the practice provides that do not entail professional fees and are an important complement to professional services. Such services could not be provided without a professional provider, usually a physician. That professional provider generates the fees for his or her professional services, but often their work expands into services that generate revenue beyond the professional component.

Ancillary services revenue is often manifested through facility and/or technical fees that the ancillary service generates. Most of these services cannot be performed without the direct involvement or, at least, the supervision of a physician or some other professional provider. PE sponsors are interested in completing an affiliation transaction that avails existing and yet-to-be-developed or realized ancillary services' sources of revenue.

This potential revenue is the "icing on the cake" which often makes a significant financial impression on the PE sponsor and then benefits the physicians in post-transaction compensation. That compensation is often realized through the *income repair* process, as discussed in Chapter 4. In fact, without these ancillary services' sources of revenue, the income repair will be delayed or insufficient to offset the *income scrape*.

STRUCTURAL EXAMPLES

When considering ancillary services, PE firms will spend much time within their due diligence processes, understanding the current ancillary services and how best to grow and expand them beyond the current state. PE firms are concerned about return on investment, but willing to supply the capital to improve upon the existing ancillary services' performance and/or to establish and invest in new services.

In a typical PE transaction with a practice or other healthcare provider, the current ancillary services are evaluated and may be assigned an appraised value along with the earnings before income taxes depreciation and amortization (EBITDA), often transcended into the *quality of earnings* analysis. The more ancillary services a practice, hospital, or other provider partner brings to the transaction, the better. Opening ancillary services revenue to the typical PE transaction is a major opportunity, especially considering the capital that many services require, as we discuss below. That capital can turn into income repair and greater value within the rollover equity invested and other expanded opportunities in the future.

Examples of such structures are often missing within existing practices due to a lack of capital to develop the ancillary services or because of legal restrictions, both tied to compliance. Restrictive covenants with health systems or other entities are also inhibitors.

In the strictest definition, ancillary services can involve joint venture initiatives and other non-clinical, non-healthcare-related investments such as real estate and medical office building developments. The typical PE transaction generally fits into the following classifications:

1. Inherent to the practice acquisition with already existing ancillary services.
2. Separate physician investments outside of the practice but capable of being included within the PE transaction (e.g., investment in the ambulatory surgery center).
3. Hospital-controlled investments where there is a willingness to partner with a third party (i.e., private equity).
4. Joint equity ventures among all participants, including PE, physicians, and hospitals/health systems.

While all these structures require meeting legal/compliance parameters, they are critical to the long-term viability of the PE transaction.

Be mindful that because ancillaries can be extremely valuable to hospitals and health systems, hospitals could seek exclusivity, as it is likely that the hospital/health system has raised or invested the financial capital necessary to complete and implement an ancillary service. Thus, they deserve to be involved, even within a PE transaction affiliation.

Such three-way deals are becoming more common, especially as physicians seek private equity for some of their affiliation solutions. Most practices do not want hospitals or health systems in which they work and with whom they have long-time relationships to abandon these associations. Therefore, a three-way ancillary investment is typical.

PE firms have been amenable to these arrangements, although they often ask the practice to dilute its equity. The practice would not dilute nor would the health system unless the health system were brought in as a third investor and would start out in the minority.

These structural examples, while broad, should be considered within every PE affiliation transaction. Exceptions would be for those specialties that rarely do work within a hospital, such as dermatology and ophthalmology. Aside from these specialties, most others would consider how best to affiliate within the ancillary services in a three-way partnership.

ANCILLARY VALUES

Private equity, as it aggregates critical masses of practices with the platform practice at the focal point, can negotiate attractive rates for these ancillary services. Often, the payers are more amenable to the private equity/practice investors, given the overall resources and capability that health systems have from inpatient and outpatient and ancillary services strength in numbers.

Hospitals negotiate better rates because of their extensive volume of services, which often transcend to ancillary services reimbursement. Therefore, the payers sometimes welcome a smaller but still strong consortium of contractual reimbursement negotiations among private equity and those practices.

Several points should be considered when reviewing ancillary services within the typical practice/PE deal, beginning with the basic earnings before income taxes depreciation and amortization (EBITDA) for each ancillary service. This factor is critical for forming the foundation for the value going forward.

If the ancillaries exist or are prospective but believed to be viable post-transaction, the PE firm often will assign a higher multiple to the overall EBITDA. This component also will reduce the income scrape since it is based on professional fees, especially if those ancillaries do not exist but are more prospective post-transaction.

Additionally, many of the ancillary services' values are based on the future expansion of those services, where the physicians are free to drive more such activity (in compliance with legal and regulatory boundaries) to the newly formed partnership (i.e., PE and practice). Driving a higher EBITDA increases the upfront payment and can be an impetus for greater ultimate value in the rollover entity.

Further, often yet-to-be or prospective ancillaries are based on a projected pro forma results post-transaction and will be "valued" in the rollover equity entity and realized (if they occur) when recapitalization results. Therefore, ancillary services offer significant opportunity and may be a major reason practices gravitate to affiliation with private equity as opposed to health systems.

Nonetheless, we believe that healthcare systems are realizing the need to partner in ancillary services development through joint equity ventures with their physicians. These partnerships are better structured under a professional services agreement (PSA) as opposed to employment and, as a result, many PSAs occur between hospitals and physician groups instead of straight employment structures.

NON-CLINICAL ANCILLARIES

As related earlier, there are opportunities to expand ancillary services beyond the most notable and predictable ones, such as those that are a part of the clinical care that physicians and other professionals provide and/or oversee. Prominent are real estate and medical office building (MOB) developments.

While there are specific regulatory and compliance boundaries upon which these joint ventures (JVs) are based, they can provide significant opportunities. Hospitals have taken advantage of this opportunity for decades as one of the more successful ancillary partnering efforts. Now, private equity is becoming involved in MOB investments and doing a credible job in formulating such ancillaries.

Real estate MOBs and other non-clinical joint investments often are capital-intensive. Physicians may be reticent to supply capital or, in many cases, do not have the liquidity to do so. Although these JVs are sometimes difficult to pull together, they are essential to the long-term adhesiveness of the association.

Three-party joint ventures are also applicable for real estate, MOBs, etc. These enterprises are interesting because they provide the "stickiness" we have suggested. Further, they offer a good return on investment, especially if the physician practices and the ancillary services themselves are performed within the MOB development. For example, if the development is supported by the services and the practice themselves, all these matters, especially the rental rates, must be within compliance boundaries with the rental rates at fair market value.

LEGAL AND REGULATORY ISSUES

Several regulatory matters should be considered. Although these regulations are discussed earlier in the book, they deserve heightened awareness as we discuss the opportunities of ancillary services and PE transactions. As a word to the wise, it is critical to use competent legal counsel with expertise in healthcare law so ancillaries are formed in compliance.

Another matter for discussion is the quality of the ancillary services delivered. Physicians must have the oversight and freedom to ensure the provision of quality care. Hospitals will offer this standard of quality because they partner with physicians, either directly or indirectly. Nonetheless, quality is usually not an issue for PE-sponsored ancillary JVs or hospitals.

SPECIFIC ANCILLARY SERVICES

When considering various specialties within the PE affiliation space, it is best to consider those most applicable to the respective specialties. Figure 8.1 illustrates the prominent physician specialties that would potentially be considered charted by various private equity firms and their typical corresponding ancillary services. This list of ancillary services is not intended to be complete. It represents only the more prominent ones.

FIGURE 8.1: Specific Ancillary Services

SPECIALTY	ANCILLARY SERVICE
Allergy	
Anesthesiology	Pain Management center
ASCs	
Cardiology	Stress testing/nuclear testing, cardio/respiratory care, catheterization laboratory
Dermatology	Retail products
Endocrinology	Nutrition education programs

FIGURE 8.1: Specific Ancillary Services (continued)

SPECIALTY	ANCILLARY SERVICE
Family Practice	X-rays, Lab, Diabetes management programs
Gastroenterology	Endoscopy center
General Surgery	ASC
Imaging/Diagnostics	
Inpatient/Hospitalist	
Internal Medicine	Lab, x-rays, Diabetes Management
Medical Oncology	
MOS Surgery	
Nephrology	Renal center
Neurosurgery	
OBGYN	
Orthopedics	X-rays, physical therapy, diagnostic center, ASC
Otolaryngology	
Pain Management	
Pediatrics	Lab, x-rays (sub-specialty may have asthma & allergy center
Plastic Surgery	ASC, Spa, Retail products
Pulmonology	Hospitalist programs, sleep study center
Radiation Oncology	
Radiology	Mammography Diagnostic Center, Invasive Radiology, Imaging centers
Surgical Oncology	
Urology	Continence center

After reviewing the general overview of the above examples, we will review the ancillaries that are especially meaningful to a private equity transaction. Keep in mind that ancillary services are equally important to health systems as they consider affiliation structures with practices of all specialties, even primary care. Health systems typically prefer that under the terms and conditions of the affiliation structure, the ancillary services will be "owned" by them.

Not surprisingly, private equity takes on the same perspective; hence, the challenges of considering both together versus completing an affiliation transaction with one, but not both.

The fiscal ramifications of including ancillaries in the affiliation structure are often the primary reason for private equity firms to pursue this type of transaction with their physician groups. Likewise, the groups have either been limited in their ability to deploy certain ancillary services due to capital, restrictive covenants, etc., and it is enticing to potentially share in that revenue stream, which has been limited, if not non-existent.

Therefore, one of the most important decisions is whether to consider ancillary income and profit that could be of use within a private equity transaction versus affiliation with a health system to entail limitations or exclusions from these investments. True, health systems can look for ways to mitigate (legally) the lack of ancillary revenue coming to the practice post-transaction. Sometimes, this can be effectuated through the overall compensation and related services' structure; however, it is a continual challenge and obstacle.

Ambulatory Surgery Centers

At the top of the list of ancillary services — and the most prized — are ambulatory surgery centers (ASCs). In many cases, a privately operated ASC, or even one that involves a health system with a minority interest, has become popular with the payers because most ambulatory centers are cost-efficient and highly productive overall within such an environment. This lower-cost ASC environment promotes private equity transactions, and the competition creates better efficiency of health systems to operate their ASCs and operating rooms.

The shift of medical care to outpatient settings has been growing for years and, while they still present certain fundamental challenges, commercial payers continue to be interested in increasing reimbursement rates for surgeries performed in an ASC. As for quality and outcomes, ASCs have historically provided high-quality results and good outcomes. This also promotes the structure of a PE transaction that includes ASCs somewhere in the overall collaborative mix.

Hospitals are responsive to ASC joint ventures with physician practices, not just because of the entry of private equity as competitors, but because hospitals have realized the benefit of cost containment, overall throughput, and structuring operations such that there is a high-level of receptivity and responsiveness within that overall structure. In other words, hospitals have realized the value that ASCs bring to working relationships and partnerships with physician groups.

Not surprisingly, patients are more satisfied with the level of care and pleased with the greater degree of flexibility in scheduling at ASCs. Many surgical procedures are elective, or at least entail some flexibility as to their scheduling and timing so they fit well within the ASC environment. This is not to say that hospital ORs and even their own ASCs are ineffective; to the contrary, ASCs and hospital ORs are essential and will continue to be critical, especially for cases.

There are opportunities to increase the overall multiple of EBITDA when ASCs are a part of the equation. Not only is this due to the increased EBITDA when considering and factoring the ASC profit potential, the mere fact that ASCs are a part of the continuum of care results in inherently greater value.

Inevitably, challenges exist in creating an ASC within a PE transaction. Many states have certificate of need (CON) requirements for approving major capital expenditures and projects for certain healthcare facilities, though these appear to be trending as less restrictive. Three-way ventures in ancillaries like ASCs are a viable possibility. Individual states' CON regulations may also affect the structure of such three-way initiatives. Usually, the PE sponsor will be brought into an existing joint venture, and thus, the physician group is required to dilute their interest, giving that minority interest to the PE sponsor. Of course, everything is negotiable.

While this is not good news to health systems and hospitals, a competitive balance of this nature is healthy and helps hospitals and health systems to look more closely at their operations, cost structures, and overall profitability of ancillary services. Growth opportunities clearly exist for all involved. We suggest a collaborative approach to the implementation, development, and ultimate growth of ancillary services among all involved parties whether it is the practice and the PE sponsor only, and/or a hospital/health system partner involved in the affiliation.

Cardiology

Similar to other specialties attracting PE interest, cardiology provides significant opportunities due to an aging population and technological advancements with the utilization of imaging ancillary services that are often performed in a physician's office. Regulatory changes relative to catheterization labs and ASCs have likewise created much interest from PE sponsors.

Many cardiologists aligned with health systems 15–20 years ago. In fact, a significant wave of hospital acquisitions of cardiologists occurred as imaging services such as nuclear studies and echocardiograms performed in the physician's office experienced a significant reduction in reimbursement from Medicare.

Because this reduction did not apply within the hospital-owned practice, many cardiologists withdrew their services in ancillaries and transferred them to hospital ownership. While this dynamic has not changed significantly, there are opportunities to work with private equity to generate critical mass volume and profits through these ancillary services.

While the ancillary services performed inside of the cardiologist's office or in the catheterization laboratory are capital-intensive, private equity can fund them and then work with the physician cardiologist regarding quality of care and overall outcomes. This is not to say that hospitals and health systems do a poor job; in fact, until recently, many of the heart catheterization and open-heart surgery procedures were completed inside the hospital and done well. The challenge is maintaining throughput and overall efficiencies inside a hospital catheterization lab or even a hospital-owned physician's office.

Cardiology will continue to be a significant element of private equity sponsorship. Many of the arrangements that cardiologists established with hospitals have expired. While this is not to say that cardiologists are unhappy with their relationship with health systems, the allurement of private equity clearly exists.

Three-way partnering between health systems, cardiology groups, and private equity is possible. There are workable models that feature these partnerships and have been successful. They should be considered as appropriate when the interest exists.

The private equity partnership opens the opportunity for more significant revenue streams through these applicable ancillary services. Medicare has added additional cardiac catheterization and coronary intervention codes to the ASC-approved list, giving even more impetus toward ancillary services with opportunities for significant fiscal opportunities.

Orthopedics

Orthopedics and related surgery initiatives such as neurosurgery are attractive specialties to investors. Several favorable market forces are in play, especially as many of these surgeries relate to sports medicine and total joint repair/replacement and recently have become almost routine. These surgeries also entail myriad ancillary services. The shift to ASCs and outpatient surgical protocols for many of these surgeries have enhanced the ancillaries that support them.

Imaging is one of the most important ancillary services supporting orthopedics and neurosurgery. From basic X-rays to CT, MRI, and related imaging procedures, they are applicable and inevitable as the surgeon diagnoses and determines how to address the patient's needs. Surgical procedures themselves continue to experience stagnant reimbursement and, in some cases, the professional and technical fees are decreasing. It is difficult for the orthopedic spine surgeon, for example, to complete a plan of care for a patient without the full continuum of ancillary services; therefore, the supporting ancillary services encompassing the entire continuum of care are essential. Orthopedic doctors often refer patients to physical and occupational therapy professionals post-surgery, to avoid surgery, or when surgery is deemed nonessential.

Pain management is related to orthopedics and neurosurgery. While a separate specialty, it is almost an ancillary in and of itself in that many orthopedic or neurosurgery patients are referred to a pain management specialist physician for care prior to or after surgery. Private equity transactions often combine all the musculoskeletal subspecialties toward the full continuum of care and the supporting ancillary services.

Regulatory and medical necessity allowances for procedures being performed in an outpatient ambulatory surgery center are becoming more common. The ancillaries that support such services are significant components of the continuum of care for patients. Therefore, it is highly unusual that an orthopedic practice would not offer these ancillaries or make them accessible through an outsourced referral.

Private equity's first strategy is to partner with an orthopedic or neurosurgery practice that has strong operational management or the ability to provide a robust array of ancillary services. This then allows for the maximization of reimbursement from all types of services, driving down competition and providing a larger overall reimbursement for those services that go to the PE sponsor and the physician partners.

Not surprisingly, private equity presents significant competitive challenges to hospitals and health systems when they not only acquire the surgical practice, but also acquire existing ancillaries or, as a strategy going forward, commit the capital to provide these services.

Three-way partnerships in certain ancillaries may be an alternative solution. The hospital or health system seeking to employ or contract with an orthopedic or neurosurgery practice via a full professional services agreement seeks all ancillary services to be provided through that health system. This assumes the ability to put together such a deal and provide sufficiently compelling economics that are also legally compliant to stimulate the physicians to accept a partnering arrangement with that health system (theoretically in deference to a private equity transaction).

Therein lie the most significant issues that hospitals and health systems have with private equity.

Other Specialties

We will not drill down on other specialties here, but suffice it to say that each one encompasses many ancillary services that supplement, if not augment, the revenue of the practice. These specialties are certainly not without capital needs, but the private equity firm usually has available funds for such. Hospitals and health systems have traditionally sought a new paradigm of private equity; practices now have choices. Thus, it bodes well for hospitals and health systems at least to consider the possibility of joint investments in ASCs, cardiology, and other ancillary services.

SUMMARY

Whether the practice specialty is gastroenterology, urology, nephrology, or myriad others, they all have critical ancillary services to consider as they review the possibilities of affiliation with private equity. No specialty is without options in how these are structured in partnership with health systems. It is difficult for all players: the practice, the private equity sponsor, and the hospitals and health system.

Is there enough revenue to go around and satisfy each practice? Time will tell, but clearly, ancillaries will continue to grow and become more significant for both private groups and private equity. They will continue to be an important revenue source for hospitals and health systems.

CHAPTER 9

The Role of MSOs and BSOs in Private Equity Deals

PRIVATE EQUITY (PE) TRANSACTIONS in the healthcare provider space often involve more than just the physician practice itself. Many deals also include separate entities known as management services organizations (MSOs) or the more recently coined business services organizations (BSOs).

MSOs and BSOs are companies that provide administrative support services to provider groups including, but not limited to, human resources, financial management and accounting services, information technology (IT) support, billing and overall revenue cycle management, compliance program management, general administrative support and oversight, and many others.

BSOs and MSOs take on similar structures and purposes, but BSOs pursue more diverse strategies than traditional healthcare administrative services, such as real estate investment, technology investment or development (i.e., business intelligence and analytics platforms), clinically integrated network (CIN) development, and clinical trials management and participation.

MSOs or BSOs are formed or included in many healthcare PE deals to maintain compliance with corporate practice of medicine (CPOM) laws. In short, CPOM laws were created to prevent or limit ownership of medical practices by individuals who are not licensed medical professionals to separate or protect clinical from commercial interests that may impact patient care.

Currently, 33 states are operating under CPOM laws, with enforcement and scrutiny varying from state to state.[1] The MSO or BSO structure allows individuals who are not licensed healthcare providers to participate in the ownership of medical practices.

The MSO or BSO also creates additional value for the PE firm by providing a separate exit opportunity for the overall entity or "platform." The role of the MSO or BSO within the PE transaction is further outlined below.

PE DEAL STRUCTURE AND MSOs OR BSOs

MSOs/BSOs within healthcare PE entities are typically formed when the initial physician practice is acquired, creating the foundation of the new platform. The MSO/BSO is formed to control all non-clinical assets of the practice, and the practice entity (often a professional corporation or PC) remains under the control of the physicians if CPOM laws apply.

If the deal is not governed by CPOM laws, then the PE firm may purchase all or some of the ownership interest in the practice. In many situations, physicians in this original platform practice may receive an equity interest in the newly formed MSO/BSO as part of the transaction.

Moving forward, the MSO/BSO provides administrative support services to the practice under a management services agreement or MSA. As the PE firm acquires more practices, commonly referred to as "add-ons," the MSO/BSO will oversee their non-clinical activities under similar MSAs.

MSAs dictate the terms of the MSO/BSO services and define the fee structure, which we will review later in this chapter. Under this structure, the goal of the PE firm is to acquire meaningful market share through add-on acquisitions while the MSO/BSO centrally manages all non-clinical aspects of the growing platform to achieve economies of scale and operational efficiency across the practices. Figure 9.1 illustrates the relationship between these parties and the flow of funds between the platform and MSO/BSO.

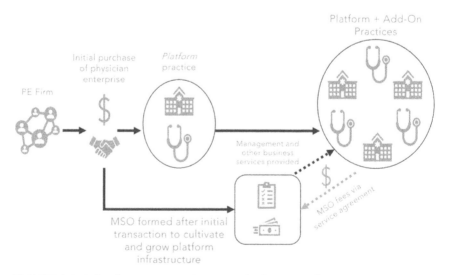

FIGURE 9.1: Role of MSOs/BSOs in PE Deals Illustrated[2]

This structure can benefit all parties involved in the following ways:[2]

PE Owners: The MSO provides a vehicle for the firm to acquire and roll up multiple practices to achieve scale. The structure offers an opportunity to leverage efficiencies and scale to improve the bottom line of the platform and, therefore, the potential exit price.

Physician Owners: Physician owners may benefit from new revenue and income opportunities provided by MSO/BSO equity interests. The aggregate scale and leverage created by the platform may afford the individual practices operational efficiencies, stronger group purchasing, and potentially more attractive commercial payer rates if the MSO/BSO is structured to provide such services.

Participating Practices: The MSO/BSO can alleviate the typical administrative burden of owning and managing a practice. If properly executed, MSO/BSO management can provide consistency to operational workflows, improve information technology capabilities and support, and offer employees more competitive fringe benefits if negotiated at the platform level.

Developing an MSO/BSO can be a critical component of PE deals in the healthcare provider space. This structure allows for aggressive growth via add-on acquisitions, which many PE firms expect, while also maintaining compliance with CPOM laws.

The next section outlines organizational structure and operational considerations for MSOs/BSOs. As an additional resource, Figure 9.2 emphasizes some of the key steps to forming MSOs/BSOs within and outside of PE deals.

MSO AND BSO STRUCTURES AND STRATEGIES

While MSOs and BSOs can vary in size and structure depending on their services offered and geographic footprint, many have organizational structures like large group practices or health systems.

The organization will have executive leadership oversight (i.e., chief executive officer, chief operating officer, chief financial officer) of departments or service lines that are supervised by directors and/or managers and structured according to the services offered to platform practices (i.e.,

FIGURE 9.2: Key Steps to Formation of MSOs/BSOs

Key Step	Description
Organizational Assessment	• Evaluate the current infrastructure supporting the services selected. • Review organizational structure needs to launch and manage services. • Determine appropriate legal structure(s) for the MSO/BSO using qualified counsel. • Develop a checklist of matters to address relative to MSO/BSO formation and execution of operations. • Develop a checklist of policies and procedures; determine current policies (if applicable) that need to be revised, and which need to be created.

Services Assessment	• Consider MSO/BSO services to offer.
	  □ Determine market demand, evaluate expertise internally, and consider outsourcing to qualified experts.
	  □ Assess the timing and roll-out of services.
	• Review current capabilities and value proposition.
	  □ Can certain services be better performed or at a lower cost than others?
	  □ Consider benchmarking analyses of key performance indicators or review market data to understand performance expectations for new services.
	  □ Is there adequate access to vendors or contractors that can provide it?

Business Planning	• Develop MSO/BSO goals. □ What does the organization want to be? Will it grow beyond local geography? Will it serve multiple specialties? Will it eventually want to exit? • Review potential fee structures for services offered. Determine which structures align with market dynamics and local/regional regulatory considerations. Develop revenue projections based on potential client base and growth scenarios. • Develop pro forma financial analyses to include anticipated revenues, expenses, capital expenditures, and growth scenarios. • Create business and strategic plans based on assessments and financial analyses. • Update business and strategic plan as needed, no less than every other year.
Marketing and Business Development	• Create materials for prospective clients or investors (e.g., pitches) that outline business and strategic plans and emphasize MSO/BSO competencies and value proposition; when needed, develop promotional materials and brochures. • Develop a list of prospective clients or investors.

FIGURE 9.2: Key Steps to Formation of MSOs/BSOs (continued)

Key Step	Description
Implementation	• Pursue the capital and infrastructure investments identified. • Create and deploy marketing and business development plans. • Hire key executive leadership if not currently in place. • Form Board and governance committees as outlined in the legal structure. • Hire additional staff, as necessary, to meet the service demands of initial clients. • Complete a thorough review of policies, procedures, and compliance programs to ensure operations and services meet regulatory standards. • Launch initial services for clients.

3-5 Year Goals and Objectives to Maximize Value	• MSO should be mindful of potential exit scenarios. While short-term priorities should include the growth and development of services, clients, owners, and investors, long-term considerations may include:
	  □ Sale of MSO to PE, insurer, health system, or other physician enterprises
	  □ Initial public offering (IPO) – less common
	  □ Merge with another MSO or BSO
	  □ Hybrid of previous options (i.e., partial sale or merger)

revenue cycle management, scheduling, credentialing, finance, patient representatives, etc.).

Additionally, MSOs and BSOs commonly have central departments that support these operational teams such as human resources, legal, compliance, and internal IT support. They may also have a board and committee structure in place for overall governance. Figure 9.3 provides an outline of these common governing bodies, as defined in a 2022 Coker whitepaper by Max Reiboldt and Andy Sobczyk.

Finally, PE firms may use local, regional, and even national MSO and BSO entities to manage large platforms for growth. In these situations, the platform may be large enough to impact commercial payer contracting for its practices (if clinically integrated) and/or leverage economies of scale for stronger group purchasing opportunities. An illustration of such an MSO or BSO platform can be found in Figure 9.4.

Another key focus area for PE firms forming MSOs or BSOs is the fee structure for services provided to platform practices. In general, there are three fee structures to consider: cost-plus, fixed-fee, and percentage of revenue.

FIGURE 9.3: Common MSO/BSO Governing Bodies[2]

Governing Body	Description
Board of Directors	• Oversees all MSO/BSO business activities. • Final approval of policies and procedures. • Creates committees of the board. • Governs membership decisions. • Approves profit distribution methodology. • Hiring and firing of an executive team.
Executive Council	• Typically composed of board officers. • Delegated authority to act on matters in between board meetings that do not require a formal board vote. • Decisions range from MSO/BSO expenditures to strategy and human resources. • Council may oversee activities of board committees.
Committees of the Board	• Board can form committees to accomplish specific organizational objectives or oversee components of MSO/BSO operations. • Committees should have a specific purpose or charter and be required to accomplish objectives on behalf of the board.

Cost-plus is a common structure as it generates a margin for the services provided and avoids the regulatory scrutiny that may come with the percentage of revenue method. PE firms may also leverage hybrid structures where fee methods vary by type of service.

MSO/BSO leadership should consult local legal counsel to understand regulations governing these fee structures. For example, percentage of revenue structures are not permitted in several states, such as New York, and may not be available to all MSOs and BSOs. More details for each method are outlined below.[2]

Cost-Plus: The MSO/BSO charges the practice for all expected costs plus a reasonable profit margin. In this approach, the key is to align actual with agreed-upon cost totals to prevent an "overrun" that could lessen the profit margin. Another way to prevent this occurrence is to retrospectively charge the practice for MSO/BSO costs to ensure a true pass-through of expense (plus the margin).

Fixed-Fee: The MSO/BSO charges the practice an annual fixed fee for the services selected. The fee reflects an agreed-upon budget with potential caveats for adjustments as warranted (e.g., increasing a practice's number of providers, additional services provided). Without an

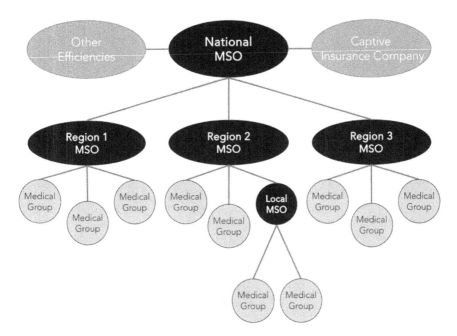

FIGURE 9.4: National MSO/BSO Structure Example[2]

allowance for such adjustments, this method is the riskiest for the MSO/ BSO to realize a profit.

Percentage of Revenue: The MSO/BSO charges the practice a percentage of net patient revenues for specific services. Such charges may be separated by service area or "bundled" as a total percentage fee. This method is also common for outsourced billing and revenue cycle providers.

In addition to organizational structure/governance and service fee considerations, PE firms that form MSOs and BSOs must also determine how to approach equity ownership. While there is no right or wrong way to structure ownership equity, leadership should pursue a method that meets the following traits and guiding principles:
- Simple and manageable.
- Equitable to all parties included in the MSO or BSO formation.
- Reasonable and legally compliant.
- Attractive to new members.
- Scalable.
- Organized in a manner that meets business plan goals and objectives.

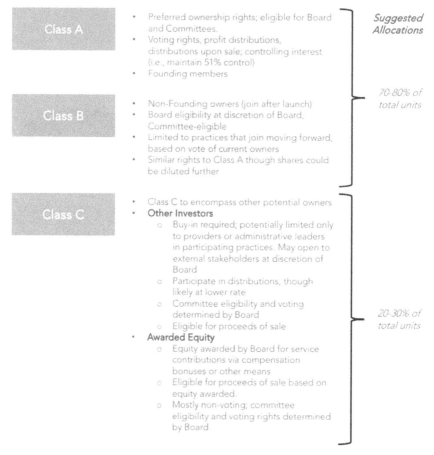

FIGURE 9.5: MSO/BSO Equity Ownership Structure Example[2]

PE firms may also choose to designate classes of equity to distinguish founding from non-founding members. Each class may have a unique set of voting rights, access to profit distributions, board and/or committee eligibility, buy-in requirements, etc.

As the primary objective of many PE platforms is growth/scale, equity structures should encourage and incentivize the addition of new members while allowing founders to maintain the appropriate or desired level of control. An example of an equity ownership structure is provided in Figure 9.5.

Organizational structure, MSO/BSO services and fees, and equity ownership are all critical decision points for PE firms as they form or acquire

FIGURE 9.6: MSO/BSO Key Steps to Operations

Key Step	Description
Performance Management	• Optimize MSO/BSO competencies and core services. Consider additional or complementary services as the organization grows (via organic growth or acquisition). Outsource services, when necessary, especially at the outset. • Determine key performance indicators (KPIs) to monitor for each service. • Evaluate the financial performance of services during the initial growth phase. • Engage physician stakeholders to develop mechanisms and provide input to the MSO/BSO (e.g., committees, governance). • Consider options for re-investing profits during the initial years. • Forgoing owner distributions during this time may be prudent to ensure the needs of the business and growth strategies can be adequately funded.

Ongoing Strategic Planning and Business Development	• Initiate ongoing strategic planning process to evaluate current services versus market needs to identify gaps and opportunities.
	  □ Consider various growth strategies beyond initial core services.
	    – Expanding the geographic footprint of practices and clients
	    – Development of clinically integrated networks; pursuit of opportunities in value-based care.
	    – Evaluate alternative lines of business or revenue sources (e.g., real estate, technology, group purchasing)
	• Accommodate new owners and investors as the ownership structure allows.
	  □ Ensure new owners and investors align with the goals of the MSO/BSO.
	• Consider the potential to acquire or develop new entities. If pursued, this strategy may warrant the development of an entity to serve as a parent company.

MSOs or BSOs. Effectively addressing these foundational elements can set the organization up for success moving forward.

Another crucial factor includes efficiently managing operations. While this chapter is more focused on the role and impact of MSOs/BSOs in PE deals, Figure 9.6 provides a summary table of key steps to managing operations for reference.

EXIT SCENARIOS

As previously mentioned, a primary objective of PE firms is to generate a return on investment (ROI), regardless of industry. Therefore, most PE transactions in healthcare will come with an expected exit strategy over a period of time. The timeframe for these exit strategies will vary depending on the goals of the fund, specialties or organizations acquired, and other market factors. As such, founders of MSOs and BSOs within healthcare PE deals may need to consider all potential exit strategies outlined below to align with the stated business objectives and expected ROI of the PE firm.

Internal organic growth: While not an "exit" strategy per se, pursuing internal organic growth simply involves optimizing current organizational performance to ensure ongoing profits and dividends for equity holders. Additionally, the MSO/BSO will continue to accrue cash holdings for potential investments and acquisitions in the future.

External investment: This strategy involves pursuing additional capital from an outside party to fuel the growth of the MSO/BSO. Pursuing external investment typically adds equity holders and may dilute current ownership shares. However, bringing in the right partners may yield stronger long-term results for the organization.

Initial public offering (IPO) potential: Pursuing an IPO is less common for healthcare MSO and BSO entities and/or PE platforms. However, it may be a viable strategy to raise significant capital for future growth, reward founding members, and generate platform awareness. Like any strategic decision, IPOs also come with risks like higher regulatory scrutiny, costs associated with public disclosures, more rigorous financial reporting, and loss of complete ownership and control of the organization.

Full sale and exit to new ownership: Selling to new ownership is a common goal of PE platforms. Aggregating physician practice assets under the "umbrella" of an MSO or BSO and then selling all or portions of the platform creates significant upside opportunities for the PE fund as well as MSO/BSO equity holders.

Hybrid scenarios: Organizations may also combine the strategies to form a more "hybrid" approach. For example, an MSO or BSO may pursue external investment in its early stage and then complete a full sale to new ownership once the platform has matured.

SUMMARY

MSOs/BSOs are often critical components of healthcare PE deals. These structures allow PE firms to aggregate assets (i.e., physician practices) under a consolidated platform while providing flexibility in how that platform is organized. Most importantly, they ensure PE deals meet regulatory guidelines in the corporate practice of medicine (CPOM) states.

Physician practice owners aligned with these platforms may have MSO or BSO equity ownership opportunities, aligning growth incentives for both the PE stakeholders and participating providers. While PE deal activity has leveled out since its peak in 2021,[3] PE stakeholders and their entities are much more relevant in the healthcare provider space than ever before. In fact, recent research conducted by the Physicians Advocacy Institute estimates that corporate-owned physician practices (which include PE platforms) make up approximately 30% of all practices, an increase of approximately 15% from 2019 to 2023.[4]

The promise of these new partnerships is still in its preliminary stages, but the rapid healthcare growth and market penetration of PE are likely to remain for some time. As such, the presence of MSOs and BSOs will continue to be felt.

REFERENCES

1. Wilmot M, Scott W, Rosenfeld E. Corporate Practice of Medicine Doctrine: Increased Enforcement on the Horizon? Nelson Mullins. January 17, 2023. https://www.nelsonmullins.com/insights/blogs/healthcare_essentials/enforcement/corporate-practice-of-medicine-doctrine-increased-enforcement-on-the-horizon.. Accessed 06-01-2024.

2. Reiboldt M, Sobczyk A. The Revival of Management Services Organizations as a Growth Strategy. Coker Whitepaper. 2022. https://assets-global.website-files.com/6596e79ed39ae84161e4c191/65eb720787c7b86d1edc0aeb_The%20Revival%20of%20MSOs%20as%20a%20Growth%20Strategy.pdf.. Accessed 06-01-2024.

3. PitchBook. Healthcare Services Report: Q1 2024. Pitchbook. May 7, 2024. Accessed June 1, 2024. https://pitchbook.com/news/reports/q1-2024-healthcare-services-report.

4. Avalere Health. . Updated Report: Hospital and Corporate Acquisition of Physician Practices and Physician Employment 2019–2023. Physicians Advocacy Institute. April 2024. Accessed June 1, 2024. https://www.physiciansadvocacyinstitute. org/Portals/0/assets/docs/PAI-Research/PAI-Avalere%20Physician%20 Employment%20Trends%20Study%202019-2023%20Final.pdf?ver=uGHF46u1G SeZgYXMKFyYvw%3d%3d.

CHAPTER 10

Affiliate Contrasts

I**N THE PREVIOUS CHAPTERS,** we discussed various factors related to private equity (PE) deals and partnerships with healthcare services entities. The focus has been on deals involving PE firms or PE-backed platforms partnering with physician enterprises because that is what we see most often in today's marketplace. From the seller's perspective, this would involve a group of physicians selling their enterprise to a PE-backed sponsor and continuing operations under that firm's majority ownership.

We should, however, take a moment to consider who the various affiliates — or buyer organizations — really are. While you, the reader, now have at least a basic understanding of what a PE firm is and how standard deals are often structured, there are facts to consider when evaluating a partnership with alternative affiliates.

PE VS. PLATFORM

First, let's examine the difference between a partnership with a PE investor and with a company (i.e., platform corporation) backed by a PE firm. A PE firm is an investment firm that raises money from institutional investors and deploys it through various investment strategies. On the other hand, a platform corporation is an existing enterprise with solid growth potential in a specific space, which a PE firm acquires as a platform investment opportunity.

This transaction has been covered previously, but because it is the first thing a seller will want to understand when considering the types of entities with whom they may partner through a transaction, it merits a review here.

Again, a PE firm is an investment firm that raises money from institutional investors (think Wall Street firms, mutual funds, family offices, endowments, pension managers); that capital is pooled into a fund from which it is deployed through various investment strategies and market sectors. Among the various kinds of investment strategies, each firm will establish investment parameters, typically tied to, for example:

- Industries or market sectors.
- Revenue and earnings before interest, taxes, depreciation and amortization (EBITDA) levels.
- Company life cycle stage (i.e., early stage, growth stage, maturity, etc.).
- Projected growth pace and other market dynamics, such as recapitalization (i.e., future sale) potential, valuation metrics, and future prospective buyer landscape.

For instance, many PE players heavily focused on the healthcare services space are in the middle market and are seeking stable targets with strong growth potential, and EBITDA potential of anywhere between $3 million to $50 million. The deal will have an ideal hold timeline of five to seven years before a recap is pursued. These general parameters are not in any way indicative of the overall PE landscape within the healthcare services space; they are, however, consistent with many of the deals having been announced in the last five or so years.

When a PE firm wants a portfolio company in a specific space, it will seek out a platform investment opportunity, meaning, it will buy an existing enterprise with strong potential for growth in that space. That initial investment will then serve as the platform on which to build and expand value through "bolt-on" investments.

A bolt-on acquisition is a company that a PE firm adds to one of its platform companies. Typically, a PE firm will partner with a larger company with a position in a particular market. This larger company becomes a platform to expand into the market because it has the management capabilities, infrastructure, and systems to allow for organic or acquisition growth.

After a hold period, the PE firm sells the overall enterprise to a larger investor who then replicates the process, although typically on a larger scale at the higher end of the overall market.

As a generalized and simplified hypothetical example, "Hypothetical Capital Partners" (HCP) is seeking to invest in the plastic surgery sector. HCP identifies various groups and pursues discussions with these targets, eventually striking a deal with "Alpha Surgical Partners" (ASP) based in Dallas, Texas. ASP is a group of 25 surgeons consisting of facial plastic surgeons, otolaryngologists (ENT), and maxillofacial surgeons, spread across four locations, with potential adjusted EBITDA estimates of approximately $12 million.

HCP and ASP solidify their deal, with ASP serving as the platform. Management is installed in collaboration with HCP and ASP, whereby the new platform then enters the market, acquiring other plastic surgery, ENT, maxillofacial, otolaryngology, and similar groups across Texas, the Southeast, and the Midwest.

After five years, ASP is sold to another investment group at a significantly higher valuation than that at which HCP originally invested in ASP. That growth in financial value, to put it simply, is how HCP achieves a significant return on investment (ROI) for its partners and investors.

The first question that a potential seller needs to ask is not necessarily, "Who do we want to partner with?" It should be, "What profile do we want in our partner? Do we want to be a platform, or should we consider joining an existing platform?" Pros and cons should be considered and evaluated when answering those questions.

Some individual owners of a physician enterprise may admit that their preference boils down to knowing who will pay the most. If they can continue delivering their services as they have historically without significant day-to-day changes, they would like to recognize some of the value they have built in their enterprise and eventually retire with their earnings.

Other individuals may place a higher emphasis on finding a longer-term partner with whom they can grow, which is often a characteristic of providers who expect to spend significant time in their professional practice.

In other cases, it might boil down to partnering with an enterprise that can help with the non-clinical functions, thus allowing the provider to focus more on their medical practice.

Often, owners want help with the operational and administrative aspects of delivering medicine, in which case an established platform may be the right choice. These are some of the qualities that should be evaluated when considering a partner.

OTHER POSSIBLE AFFILIATES

These standard types of PE deals are not the only alternatives available. When we are working with a group seeking a sale of their enterprise, we encourage them to at least consider several potential partners. Who are these potential partners?

We first suggest at least considering partnering with a hospital or health system; existing dynamics between most groups and their local or regional hospital organizations make this an obvious first choice.

Of course, for some groups or certain specialties, this alternative simply is not realistic or feasible, in which case, at least, we took that alternative off the table. There have been numerous situations where we made this suggestion, and while it was met with negativity, in the end, it turned out there was indeed a competitive and attractive opportunity that the group had otherwise not considered.

For example, we were advising a large OB/GYN group that was contemplating a partnership with a PE sponsor, primarily as a bolt-on investment within an existing platform. The leadership was under the assumption that for a group their size and with their specialty, this was their best alternative at the time.

We also were advising their main hospital partner; the hospital partner was also interested in an affiliation with the group, which was the largest partnered OB services provider within their system. The group's leadership was assuming the health system would not be able to pay the same value as a PE-backed platform.

Through negotiation, we were able to develop a deal structure that would indeed achieve a desired valuation while continuing to deliver compelling downstream value to the providers; it was structured in a manner that met the rigid regulatory requirements that govern such affiliations. The lesson is that it is wise to properly consider and evaluate all alternatives before making a decision.

Although there are various types of affiliates, most will fall into one of the categories of affiliates previously described. Sometimes, however, hybrid deals can be made. We advised a large group that did a simultaneous transaction whereby they sold a portion of the group's services to a PE firm while entering into a professional services agreement (PSA) with the main hospital partner. This arrangement allowed the PE partner to achieve value through certain ancillaries, while the hospital could continue to partner with the providers on the professional fee and hospital-based services and procedures.

That particular group has since recapped multiple times with various capital partners while maintaining their partnership with the hospital; that hospital has gone on to participate in other similarly structured multi-party transactions in other specialties.

We have been involved in other structured deals too. Sometimes real estate was a component; the group might partner with one party on the enterprise side of the deal while partnering with a real estate investor on the property side. Joint ventures are an alternative that calls for a group to engage in a joint venture (JV) on specific carved-out services (ancillaries, for instance) while selling the rest of their enterprise in a PE-backed deal. Diverse types of JVs have occurred for decades, especially in areas such as imaging, pathology lab services, ambulatory surgery centers (ASCs), and other groups that extend beyond standard professional and surgical services; this is uncommon for multi-party deals involving private equity-sponsored transactions.

Management services organizations (MSOs) and similar platforms, which we have covered in other chapters, can also present an opportunity for consideration regarding potential affiliation partners. Rarely is there a single way to structure any given deal, and new types are being structured in this space all the time.

SUMMARY

Potential sellers should be open to considering all alternatives and evaluate all options before choosing one path. Although in some cases, a single pathway will be clear, all possibilities should be identified and explored. One never knows when a previously undiscovered pathway might lead to a greater probability of achieving desired goals and outcomes.

CHAPTER 11

Specialty Nuances

As we have discussed in previous chapters, private equity is becoming increasingly popular across all areas of U.S. healthcare markets. If a practice is financially strong and offers an ability to grow within its existing market, a case can be made for private equity.

That said, certain specialties have attracted more attention from investors due to their potential return on investment. In this chapter, we will detail the nuances of private equity across specific types of practice settings and specialty categories.

THE CONSOLIDATION CURVE

As we consider private equity within various specialties, it is important to understand the overall trajectory of consolidation in the industry. Accordingly, we reference "The Consolidation Curve" throughout, which is depicted in Figure 11.1.[1]

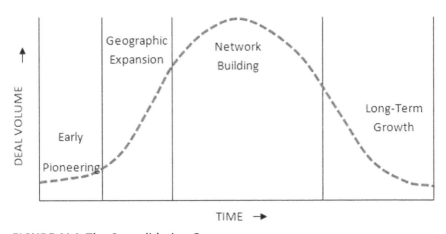

FIGURE 11.1: The Consolidation Curve

As with other business life cycles, specific specialties fall within various portions of The Consolidation Curve.

A 2022 study by The National Institute for Health Care Management (NIHCM) found that preliminary private equity transactions were concentrated in the Northeast, Florida, and Arizona.[2] However, in recent years, as organizations enter the geographic expansion phase of The Consolidation Curve, practices are being acquired in tangential and complimentary markets.

As discussed in previous chapters, there are often "platform practices" that form the foundation of a regional presence, with the private equity firm then considering "add-ons" of a smaller scale. These deals typically result in less significant multiples, but still offer strong returns. Within The Consolidation Curve, this is considered the network-building phase.

HOSPITAL- AND CONTRACT-BASED SPECIALTIES

The first specialties we consider are organizations that support hospital services but are often managed distinctly from hospitals themselves, such as anesthesiology, radiology, and emergency medicine. Private equity has focused significantly on these services, consolidating these organizations rapidly and creating highly scaled operations. Most of these specialties fall within the long-term growth phase of The Consolidation Curve.

Anesthesiology

Anesthesia has a unique advantage for private equity firms. It is a high-profit margin specialty with a clear buyer, such as hospitals and ambulatory surgery centers (ASC). Further, anesthesia services are in high demand, with providers' salaries increasing and creating challenges for remaining independent anesthesia practices.

Further, much of the anesthesia market was already consolidated via physician management companies due to the challenges of staffing and scheduling, revenue cycle management complexities, and comprehensive contracts with hospitals. Thus, private equity could make considerable transactions and assume existing scale versus having to cobble together independent practices.

According to a 2020 *Journal of the American Medical Association* (JAMA) Network study, anesthesia practice made up approximately 20% of the private equity transactions from 2013 to 2016, resulting in approximately 33% of anesthesiologists employed by a private equity-backed organization.[3]

One such private equity-backed firm, U.S. Anesthesia Partners, is being sued by the Federal Trade Commission (FTC) for creating a monopoly in Texas. The FTC has cleared the private equity partner, Welsh, Carson, Anderson & Stowe, of wrongdoing; however, U.S. Anesthesia Partners is still under review. While this case is ongoing at the time of publication of this book, we note that although this may cause pause for some organizations, we do not expect transactions in the anesthesia space to cease altogether.

Key Players in the Anesthesia Market:
- U.S. Anesthesia Partners
- North American Partners in Anesthesia
- NorthStar Anesthesia

Radiology

Radiology has many of the same features as anesthesia and has seen similar interest. In a study completed by Health Affairs in 2024, the number of private equity-backed practice sites for radiology increased 608% from 2012 to 2021 (816 to 5,779).[4] Further, radiology practices account for approximately 4.4% of all private equity transactions throughout the industry.

Radiology has become an increasingly important specialty in the overall care delivery system. When considering that, compounded with the cost of staying relevant with the latest technologies, it is clear why private equity has made radiology a focus.

It is important to note that the same firm that was accused by the FTC of creating a monopoly in anesthesia, Welsh, Carson, Anderson & Stowe, was also accused of doing so for radiology via U.S. Radiology Specialists. While this case was also dismissed, we point out the increasing focus of the FTC on these types of cases and the general oversight of transactions. Regardless, we expect radiology to remain a competitive specialty in the private equity space.

Key Players in the Radiology Market:
- Radiology Partners
- U.S. Radiology Specialists

Emergency Medicine

Finally, we consider emergency medicine under these contract-based specialties, which potentially is the most concentrated specialty for private equity. PE-backed physician staffing groups operate nearly one-third of emergency departments in the United States according to documentation from Senator Gary Peters, D-Mich., who currently is chair of the Senate's Homeland Security Committee. Further, according to a study by a group presenting at ASHEcon in 2020, 11.3% of all emergency medicine practices were owned by private equity firms in 2019, with significant concentration in just a few firms.[5]

The main attraction for private equity in emergency medicine is the availability of staffing across the country, with firms seeking a blended approach to care that shifts to higher utilization of advanced practice providers (APPs). Regardless, this answers the question for many hospitals over coverage, ensuring adequate staffing of a necessary resource.

Again, we note that there are current probes into the concentration of private equity in emergency medicine. We expect to see changes in the market related to emergency medicine as these investigations conclude.

Key Players in the Emergency Medicine Market:
- Apollo Global Management
- Blackstone Group
- KKR

Non-Hospital-Affiliated Specialties

The next practice settings we consider are specialties not typically associated with hospital entities, including dermatology, ophthalmology, and dental practices. These types of specialties remained highly fragmented, protected from the rapid consolidation and employment by hospitals seen in other specialties. Thus, these practices were some of the earliest to be targeted by private equity and remain among the most popular specialties for private equity firms. Generally, these are in the network-building phase of The Consolidation Curve.

Dermatology

Dermatology was one of the first specialties to attract private equity attention, with firms completing deals in this space for decades. As of March 2023, a *Journal of Drugs in Dermatology* study indicated that 10%–15% of all dermatology practices were backed by private equity, with expected continuation of investment.[6]

Dermatology stood out due to the rising demand for both cosmetic and skin cancer services, the aging population (and resulting increased demand for services) in the United States, and the specialty's unique opportunity to generate returns.

Based on studies completed in the specialty, dermatology reached somewhat of a peak in 2018; however, it remains a compelling market, with significant remaining opportunities to expand.

Key Players in the Dermatology Market:

- Aqua Dermatology
- Advanced Dermatology and Cosmetic Surgery
- Anne Arundel Dermatology
- Dermatologists of Central States
- Dermatology Medical Partners
- Epiphany Dermatology
- Forefront Dermatology
- Hidden Harbor Capital Partners
- QualDerm Partners
- United Derm Partners
- US Dermatology Partners

Ophthalmology

Similar to dermatology, ophthalmology has proved to be a highly attractive market for private equity since the early 2010s, with a concentration of transactions in 2017. As of 2022, the president of the American Academy of Ophthalmology (AAO), Robert Wiggins Jr., MD, reported that 8% of ophthalmologists work in a private equity-backed practice.[7]

Again, we emphasize the importance the aging population plays in driving increased demand for ophthalmology across the country, creating a strong market for investment. As with other specialties, there remains a significant shortage of physicians, which only furthers the supply/demand analysis considered by private equity.

These transactions encompass all components of the ophthalmic space, with investors seeking practices specializing in retina, vision, and comprehensive services. Thus, we do not see these acquisitions slowing in future years but continuing into the expansion phase of private equity transactions.

Key Players in the Ophthalmology Market:
- Advancing Eyecare
- Ascend Vision Partners
- Blue Point Capital Partners
- EyeCare Partners
- EyeSouth Partners
- Prism Vision Group
- Retina Consultants of America
- Sight360
- Unifeye Vision Partners
- Vision Integrated Partners

Dental

As with dermatology and ophthalmology, dental practices have been targeted by private equity, with much of the investment focused on dental management services organizations. This dates to the 1990s, with the inception of Aspen Dental and picking up in the 2010s. Specifically, a study by Eileen O'Grady of Private Equity Stakeholder Project in 2023 indicated that private equity firms owned 27 of the top 30 dental services organizations.[8]

Dental practices offer an opportunity for private equity firms to build scale quickly and create cost efficiencies. These practices are better equipped to have a large geographical or even national presence, creating a unique opportunity in the market. Further, dental revenue has continued to grow in recent years, creating further opportunities for investors.

While dental acquisitions may have seen their peak, we believe we are just entering the phases of secondary sales, which will continue to consolidate the market. Over one hundred active dental services organizations are in the market, with continual growth in the marketplace; therefore, it remains a highly active specialty for acquisitions and consolidation.

Key Players in the Dental Market:
- Aspen Dental
- Dental Care Alliance

- Heartland Dental
- MB2 Dental
- Smile Brands

OTHER SPECIALTY PRACTICES

Next, we consider more standard specialty practices, including many that have been targeted by hospitals for acquisition as well. While these were pursued later by private equity, they have become increasingly popular in recent years, offering a unique opportunity to practices that have remained independent. Thus, these are mostly in the geographic expansion phase of The Consolidation Curve.

While this can include all remaining specialties, we consider a few specific and popular ones below. Overarchingly, the specialties that are most interesting to private equity are those that have significant revenue related to drugs and/or ancillaries, creating a potential for greater profit margins.

Gastroenterology

Gastroenterology is the second most concentrated specialty for private equity acquisitions, behind dermatology. Interest in gastroenterology began in 2016, but has quickly picked up steam, with rapid expansion between 2019 and 2021 and continuing to the present day. Specifically, in 2021, the number of transactions in the gastroenterology space increased by 28%, with a focus on "add-on" practices.[9]

One of the key reasons gastroenterology has been targeted by private equity is due to the increased interest and need for colonoscopies. The United States has an aging patient population, which is creating additional demand for these procedures. Further, the Centers for Disease Control and Prevention recently lowered the recommended age for these screenings to 45.[10] Thus, gastroenterology is an excellent strategic choice for private equity, offering high-volume procedures with further room for growth. Additionally, endoscopy centers often drive higher multiples, offering an attractive investment opportunity.

While significant platform practice exists, there is still room in the market for "add-on" practices. Further, as the firms continue to look to expand geographically, there remains potential for additional platform practices in new markets.

Key Players in the Gastroenterology Market:

- Unio Health Partners
- Covenant Physician Partners
- Gastro Care Partners
- The GI Alliance
- Gastro Health
- One GI
- Gastro MD
- United Digestive
- Capital Digestive Care
- Allied Digestive Health
- US Digestive Health
- Pinnacle GI Partners

Urology

Urology closely follows gastroenterology in terms of private equity interest. Urology became increasingly popular in 2020, with significant volumes of transactions in the years following.

As with other specialties mentioned in this chapter, the popularity of urology is driven mostly by increasing demand, including factors related to the aging population and ongoing physician shortage. Urology has unique factors that drive the value proposition, including strong ancillary revenues and participation in surgery centers.

Urology is still relatively closely held, with seven private equity firms dominating the market; thus, we expect to see new entrants as the specialty expands in interest.

Key Players in the Urology Market:

- Atlas Urology
- Solaris Health
- Summit Health
- Unio Health Partners
- United Urology Group
- Urology America
- US Urology Partners

Women's Health

Women's health specialties, including OB/GYN, fertility, and maternal-fetal medicine, have become increasingly popular for private equity transactions in recent years. Like other specialties, initial private equity deals in the women's health space started almost 10 years ago, but after 2020, deal volumes increased exponentially.

Women's health has increased in significance due to a range of factors, including the advancing age of mothers (and related needed care), ancillary services, and value-based care expectations. Thus, this comprehensive specialty creates a strong investment opportunity. Additionally, investors are seeking to capitalize on the advancements in fertility treatments, including expanding overage (both by private and government programs).

Currently, there are a few dominant players in the market, but this is expected to keep expanding as women's health progresses in consolidation efforts.

Key Players in the Women's Health Market:
- Advantia Health
- Axia Women's Health
- Femwell Group Health
- The Women's Health Group
- Together Women's Health
- Unified Women's Healthcare
- Women's Care Enterprises

Orthopedics

Orthopedics became prominent in the private equity space in 2021, rapidly expanding the number of transactions in 2022 and beyond. It is now one of the top six specialties targeted for such transactions, creating significant density throughout the market.

As with other specialties, orthopedics is highly attractive due to the increasing demand and mitigated supply. As the population ages, orthopedic procedures such as hip and knee replacements are rapidly increasing. Many orthopedic practices have highly profitable surgery centers with strong ancillary volumes, which can also serve as a strong investment proposition for organizations.

As of 2023, there were eighteen private equity-backed orthopedic platforms, with firms focusing on add-on opportunities and geographic expansion.[10]

Key Players in the Orthopedic Market:
- Healthcare Outcomes Performance Company (HOPco)
- Orthopedic Care Partners
- United Musculoskeletal Partners
- U.S. Orthopaedic Partners

Oncology

Oncology is another recent specialty that has received attention from private equity, first gaining traction in 2018. A study by *JAMA* in 2023 indicated that 724 oncology clinics were acquired by private equity from 2003 to 2022, constituting approximately 10% of all oncology clinics in the U.S. Of those, 53% were radiation, 32% were medical, and 15% were multi-oncologic.[11]

Oncology is unique in its market offerings, given the potential to capitalize on expensive injections and drugs. This creates significant revenue streams and the potential to scale the businesses across markets.

The same *JAMA* study referenced above identified 23 private equity-backed platform companies, with 10 of those being acquired by another private equity-backed entity or public company.[11]

Key Players in the Oncology Market:
- American Oncology Network
- Cancer Treatment Centers of America
- Integrated Oncology Network
- Oncology Care Partners
- OneOncology
- The Oncology Institute of Hope and Innovation
- The US Oncology Network
- Verdi Oncology

Cardiology

Potentially the newest specialty to gain traction, cardiology, has seen a significant increase in deal volumes in the last two years. As this is still relatively new, most continue to be platform acquisitions with focused regional footprints.

Like urology, the key driver for this market is the high volume of procedures and ancillary volumes, with room for growth. As of 2020, CMS added percutaneous coronary interventions to the list of ASC-covered procedures. Thus, there has been an influx in revenues attributed to private practices that own ASCs.

Again, this specialty has gained momentum and, therefore, will continue to see engagement in future years.

Key Players in the Cardiology Market:
- Cardiovascular Associates of America
- National Cardiovascular Partners
- US Heart & Vascular

FUTURE SPECIALTIES

The newest forefront of private equity is focused on primary care models. As indicated above, the focus of private equity in the early 2010s and 2020s was mostly on procedural specialties with high margins and volumes. Moving into 2024 and beyond, there is increased interest in primary care, internal medicine, and pediatrics.

Private equity is seeing the benefit in targeting larger networks of providers and retaining referrals within these networks, thus generating profits from the ancillary and procedural referrals related thereto. Further, as value-based care continues to become more prominent, there are significant opportunities for organizations that can harness volume and manage their populations well.

In this aspect, the biggest component for private equity investors in these new specialties is scale. While this is relevant for all specialties, it is critical in primary care. Additionally, these are often bolted onto existing specialty platforms to manage those referrals in the most effective way. As this is still a newer area for transactions, we expect to see ongoing increases in deal activity, including platform practice purchases and add-on practices.

Key Players in the Primary Care Market:
- Agilon Health

- Privai Health
- One Medical
- Village MD

Additional information is available in Appendix A, Examples of Private Equity Firms and Associated Specialties.

SUMMARY

Throughout this chapter, we have discussed the nuances of private equity transactions by specialty, and yet, much of the core premises remain the same. Investors are seeking practices with the potential to consolidate in markets, expand their footprint and volumes, and ensure high margins.

As organizations consider potential partnerships, it is important to understand where their specialty falls within the timeline of transactions and within The Consolidation Curve. Additionally, it is critical to ensure the practice highlights the key metrics that are attractive to investors by specialty (i.e., volumes, referral base, panel size, ASC ownership, etc.).

Finally, organizations should research what other deals have been done for their specialty in the area and determine if there is still the opportunity to be acquired as a platform practice or if a transaction would be structured as an add-on.

REFERENCES

1. Yetter E. Private Equity's Medical Practice Consolidation Curve. Where Different Specialties Lie. FOCUS Investment Banking. Accessed June 9, 2024. https://focusbankers.com/private-equitys-medical-practice-consolidation-curve-where-different-specialties-lie/.

2. Singh Y, Zhu JM, Polsky D, Song Z. Geographic Variation in Private Equity Penetration Across Physician Specialties. NIHCM Foundation. Accessed June 10, 2024. https://nihcm.org/publications/geographic-variation-in-private-equity-penetration-across-physician-specialties.

3. Zhu JM, Hua LM, Polsky D. Private Equity Acquisitions of Physician Medical Groups Across Specialties. JAMA. 2020; 323(7):663–665. Accessed June 10, 2024. doi:10.1001/jama.2019.21844. https://jamanetwork.com/journals/jama/fullarticle/2761076.

4. Abdelhad O, Fulton BD, Alexander L, Scheffler RM. Private Equity—Acquired Physician Practices and Market Penetration Increased Substantially, 2012-21.

Health Affairs. 2024;42(3). Accessed June 10, 2024. https://doi.org/10.1377/hlthaff.2023.00152.

5. Adler L, Nikpay SS. The Proliferation of Private Equity in Emergency Medicine and Anesthesiology and Its Effects. 2020 ASHEcon Virtual Conference Agenda. June 8, 2020. Accessed June 9, 2024. https://ashecon.confex.com/ashecon/2020/meetingapp.cgi/Paper/9968.

6. Sung CT, Salem S, Oulee A, *et al.* A Systematic Review: Landscape of Private Equity in Dermatology from Past to Present. *J Drugs Dermatol.* 2023;22(4):404-408. Accessed June 10, 2024. doi:10.36849/JDD.6892. https://jddonline.com/articles/a-systematic-review-landscape-of-private-equity-in-dermatology-from-past-to-present-S1545961623P0404X.

7. Wehrwein P. Private Equity, Boon or Bane, for Retina Specialists? *Managed Healthcare Executive.* November 4, 2023. Accessed June 11, 2024. https://www.managedhealthcareexecutive.com/view/private-equity-boon-or-bane-for-retina-specialists-aao-2023.

8. O'Grady E. *Deceptive Marketing, Medicaid Fraud, and Unnecessary Root Canals on Babies: Private Equity Drills into the Dental Care Industry.* Private Equity Stakeholder Project. Accessed June 11, 2024. https://pestakeholder.org/wp-content/uploads/2021/08/PESP_DSO_July2021.pdf.

9. *The Business of Gastroenterology Quarterly Newsletter | Q4 2021.* Spherix Global Insights/Fraser Healthcare. 2024. Accessed June 11, 2024. https://secureservercdn.net/166.62.107.20/bpl.670.myftpupload.com/wp-content/uploads/2022/02/Special-Topix_The-Business-of-Gastroenterology-US_Newsletter-Q4-2021-FINAL.pdf.

10. Kinkaid G. 45 Is the New 50 for Colorectal Cancer Screening. Centers for Disease Control and Prevention. June 8, 2021. Accessed June 14, 2024. https://blogs.cdc.gov/cancer/2021/06/08/45-is-the-new-50-for-colorectal-cancer-screening/.

11. Tyan K, Lam MB, Milligan M. Private Equity Acquisition of Oncology Clinics in the US From 2003 to 2022. *JAMA Internal Medicine.* 2023;183(6): 621-623. https://doi.org/10.1001/jamainternmed.2023.0334

CHAPTER 12

Conclusions Regarding Private Equity Deals

A S WE CONCLUDE THIS BOOK and reflect on the chapters' content, we will discuss some key takeaways. While the information in this chapter is a summary of the matters touched on earlier, given the level of uncertainty and volatility of healthcare entities and private equity (PE) affiliation, there are several essential points to consider.

CRITICAL CHARACTERISTICS OF PE-BACKED FIRMS AND HEALTHCARE ENTITY AFFILIATION

The three significant areas of consideration with all affiliation deals are *structure, economics, and governance.* No matter the parties involved, these three areas must be considered for a healthcare entity transaction. As to PE-backed firms, the specificities of structure, economics, and governance differ from when healthcare providers such as medical practices align with healthcare systems to include hospitals and related entities. Nevertheless, similarities abound.

Still, some fundamental differences exist between PE-firm-backed transactions and healthcare providers. We have presented and discussed these differences in earlier chapters but delineate the vital aspects as we summarize this book.

Key Similarities

As we consider the similarities between PE and other healthcare entity affiliations, there are some notable points of common ground. These include:

1. Mutual emphasis on continuing to maintain quality care.
2. Motivation for realizing a profit margin and return on investment (ROI).
3. Desire for ancillary services development and/or growth and resultant ROI.

4. Accurate and compliant valuation and/or quality of earnings (QofE) economic foundations.
5. Desire for cost and volume efficiency.
6. Emphasis on growth and expansion after transaction.
7. Necessity of retaining providers and probability of recruiting additional providers.
8. Compensation of providers, both competitive and realistic.

Key Differences

Along with the similarities, there are several key differences between typical PE transactions and other forms of affiliation among healthcare providers. These include:

1. Valuation derived accurately via a market approach as opposed to cost or income approaches. Additionally, the derivation is usually through a QofE analysis, not a valuation or appraisal, per se.
2. Post-transaction compensation that entails the income scrape used to derive EBITDA.
3. Shorter-term affiliation, meaning inevitably, the PE firm will undergo a recapitalization in approximately five years.
4. Future affiliation that is short, not inherently long-term, nor is it intended as such.
5. Physicians as investors, including investing in rollover equity.
6. Varied benefits post-transaction, including those for the providers.
7. Support via a management services organization (MSO) entity.
8. Recruitment and retention applied with a shorter-term goal.
9. All assets of affiliation aimed at a short-term relationship.
10. Not especially concerned about a continuum of care outside its services.

Next, let us review some of the key components of the three major areas of getting a PE-backed firm deal completed with a healthcare entity.

ECONOMICS

The economics of PE deals entail several key concepts and terms (see Appendix D). Several buzzwords are:

- *Income scrape.* This is a reduction of physician compensation to create earnings on which a multiple is applied to derive the upfront dollars paid by a PE-backed deal.
- *Income repair.* This includes efforts to offset the income reductions through increased cost efficiencies, managed care contracting, reimbursement improvements, etc.
- *EBITDA.* The earnings on which the healthcare entity's value is based are largely attributable to that valuation or QofE process.
- *Rollover equity.* Unlike other healthcare provider transactions, PE almost always requires reinvestment in a new company called *Newco*. The *Newco* is part of what would otherwise be the proceeds from the sale of the practice/healthcare entity.
- *Second bite of the apple.* This process is the recapitalization that inevitably occurs when the PE firm chooses to sell its interest. That *second bite* is a result of the recapitalization and hopefully a second *closing* of some value to the physicians or other healthcare entity investors.
- *Multiples.* These equivocate to market rates to derive the total value when multiplied by EBITDA. The multiples can vary based on the QofE analysis and market conditions, even the specialty and type of healthcare entity under consideration. For example, an ASC may call for a higher multiple than the practice alone.
- *Platform.* The platform is the practice formed by the PE transaction that entails the basis upon which the private entity will complete additional merger and acquisition (M&A) work to build around that foundational practice entity.
- *IOI and LOI.* In addition, the indication of interest (IOI) and letter of intent (LOI) are tools used to expound upon the PE entity's initial offers to acquire the healthcare entity. While not legally binding, they are expected to be the basis on which a deal is finalized.

STRUCTURE

The PE deal structure entails the framework of the economics and related terms and conditions outlined above. It is almost always a purchase and subsequent employment by the MSO subsidiary of the PE sponsor or directly by an owner tied to the PE firm. While physicians invest in the rollover entity and have equity in the same, they possess minority interests and do not have actual voting or even income distribution rights in most cases. The *payday* for rollover investments comes when the recapitalization and subsequent sale (likely to another PE firm) is consummated, typically five to seven years later.

Other structural elements include a possibility of investments in ancillary services, but usually these are reserved for the PE sponsor/employer. While the practice may continue to operate similarly in day-to-day operations, decision-making, etc., the PE-backed firm is in ultimate control as the majority owner. Thus, the structure does not include professional services agreements (PSAs) per se (i.e., IRS-1099 contractual arrangements), which are becoming more popular in affiliation transactions among physicians and healthcare systems.

GOVERNANCE

The third major component of a deal is governance and related decision-making. Governance calls for parameters and boundaries of decision-making and related leadership of the practice/healthcare entity post-transaction.

Keep in mind that the PE firm, as the majority owner, is the ultimate decision-maker. However, depending on the structure and the PE firm's desire for leadership and governance, they may allow the practice or other healthcare entity being acquired to continue fulfilling these roles on a day-to-day basis. Certain *reserved powers* may be established for ultimate control/supervision. The administrative management of the practice/healthcare entity being acquired by PE could be in the form of an MSO, although this is not always necessary. State laws relative to physician practice ownership may require the MSO structure.

RECOMMENDED ATTITUDE TOWARD PE — PRACTICE OR HEALTHCARE PROVIDER PERSPECTIVES

With the above areas of consideration in mind, the following are some key action items a healthcare entity considering PE affiliation should apply. These are imperative to decide not only whether to affiliate with PE but also if to proceed with a specific PE firm.

1. *Explore.* Explore the options and understand how PE works.
2. *Educate.* Much of the PE process is tied to physicians' and other owners' full understanding of the structure, organizational makeup, economics, and other matters relative to the typical PE transaction. Therefore, educating the decision-makers, many of whom are not businesspeople with inherent knowledge of how such things work, is essential.
3. *Strategize.* Develop a strategy that allows for a process, not only of education but also as decisions are made, to pursue PE to be put into a solid strategic plan.
4. *Consider the pros and cons.* We have not expressed any leanings for or against PE transactions with healthcare providers; rather, we have presented the pluses and minuses throughout the book. Medical practices and other healthcare organizations likewise should assume this approach. Take a cautionary view by not being too quick for or against a PE transaction. With an open mind, strive to understand through exploration, education, and strategizing when considering a potential decision.
5. *Evaluate risks versus rewards.* Any transaction involving significant organizational changes should include a risk-reward assessment, which applies to private equity, as well.
6. *Pursue as complete.* It is often said that a party, such as a healthcare provider organization, may only superficially consider private equity (PE) investment, also known as "kicking tires," without serious intent. This is acceptable if the party is simply seeking education and gathering information, but not if they have no real interest in pursuing PE.
7. *Obligate.* Undertaking a PE transaction involves commitment, especially after the initial education and fact-finding stages are completed. The parties involved do not need to commit to a specific obligation at the beginning of the process; however, at some point, they must decide how serious they are about moving forward.
8. *Consider all providers' points of view.* Our emphasis throughout these chapters is that no PE transaction is perfect, and none will completely satisfy all the physician owners. Thus, all viewpoints should be carefully considered with the help of an independent adviser to compile

those concerns and build consensus for a decision to arrive at a "go" or "no go" decision.

9. ***Review the options.*** We recommend that practices complete the guidelines noted above (such as education about the typical PE deal) and look at other options available to them. For example, health systems are usually interested in most specialties and will carefully consider affiliation instead of the PE option.

10. ***Differentiate.*** It is important to spell out the varying dynamics for both private equity at large and individual PE firms pursuing a healthcare organization. It is essential to be able to sort through the differences, both positive and negative factors, of the various PE sponsors. Remember, if you go with PE, it will be one of the final affiliation decisions you make, at least for a while, relative to affiliation. You should not look back. Be able to differentiate one PE firm from another, their deal structure, culture, what they will allow or not post-transaction.

CHALLENGES INVOLVING HOSPITALS

PE transaction considerations present many challenges. As a review, let's consider the most prominent ones involving hospitals, which may create, or even prevent, what would otherwise be a successful PE transaction based on their overall control and resources within the market.

1. ***Referral sources.*** Practices, especially specialty practices, often hesitate to complete a PE transaction to which the PE partner undoubtedly adds ancillary services. The potential risk is the drying up of referral sources. Many hospitals, for example, control most primary care providers and thus can limit referrals or even potentially recruit other specialty physicians in competition.

2. ***Specialty-specific recruitment.*** As suggested above, this is a challenge in which hospitals may recruit to build their own specialty base and not consider the PE-aligned specialty practice(s).

3. ***Older versus younger physicians.*** Physicians with years left to practice and those near retirement have different points of view relative to PE. Hospitals offer a viable alternative, especially to older physicians; younger ones who do not have trepidation of being affiliated with health systems are a factor. By the same token, some older physicians

are amenable to finishing their careers under an employment or professional services agreement (PSA) model of hospitals.

4. *Ancillary services requirements*. As noted previously, ancillaries are a major consideration of PE. Most of the alignment structures between hospitals and private groups assume health systems have a responsibility and reimbursement for most, if not all, the ancillaries. This presents a tremendous challenge when PE is involved. PE firms want those ancillary services as a part of their overall continuum and partnership with the practices. Depending on the legal and other matters, this could create a significant challenge to overcome in that the hospitals will control those ancillaries.

5. *Recruitment and retention*. Hospitals typically contribute significantly to recruitment and retention, which they conduct within legal parameters, especially when structuring income guarantees, etc. While PE makes a commitment to both recruitment and retention, they typically do not have the tools available to health systems. Therefore, recruitment and retention can be challenging when hospitals present more compelling offers.

6. *Income repair*. PE asserts income repair, and rightfully so. This is challenging, especially with hospital competition that will increase once a practice aligns if a practice aligns with PE instead of the hospital.

7. *Overall hospital competition*. Practices that align with PE must expect to some degree that hospitals have become their competitors and vice versa. While we do not subscribe to this view, it is a definitive factor to consider, even if it is challenging for practices to align with PE.

8. *For-profit mindset*. Having a for-profit mindset and still being legally compliant as a not-for-profit entity is often the case with health systems that are indeed tax-exempt. Therefore, they create similar competitive challenges. Hospitals are more open to PSA structures than full-fledged employment, thereby creating additional challenges for PE to convince a practice affiliate.

9. *Due diligence process*. Hospitals and PE groups complete due diligence when closing transactions with groups, although hospitals work on a more streamlined, independent basis, whereas PEs determine a specific period, such as 60–90 days, to complete a more comprehensive due diligence process. If issues are discovered during

due diligence, PE will often adjust the purchase price downward or upward.

CHALLENGES REGARDING GROUP MERGERS AND PE DEALS

We will also point out the challenges that PE transactions may present:

1. *Control of future direction consensus.* Remember, the PE sponsor and/or MSO becomes the majority owner. Therefore, there are definite differences of opinion and processes from the previous healthcare organization, which usually was controlled by physicians.

2. *Income distribution plan (IDP).* The IDP post-transaction is often left up to the practice, but PE sets the parameters relative to the income scrape and the potential mitigation of the IDP through income repair.

3. *Post-merger governance and leadership.* Often, PE will leave recently purchased practices and other healthcare entities alone to practice and make most of the operational decisions post-transaction. These are day-to-day decisions and not "major, big picture" ones. Furthermore, reserved powers are set aside for the PE sponsor to control.

4. *Value extraction ability.* By this, we mean how much value PE can extract from the practice and the challenges created for it. This relates to some of the factors discussed above and below.

5. *Ancillaries.* Not surprisingly, ancillaries are a major consideration and could be an obstacle if those ancillaries remain primarily within the hospital.

6. *Physical location.* While PE usually leaves a practice or other healthcare organization at its current physician locations, there could be and often are some duplicative structures, especially when practices and other entities are added within the platform. The practice and often its physician landlords may lose this rental income source.

7. *Real estate considerations.* Akin to the previous point, real estate is often owned by practices (i.e., their physicians and separate entities, not the practice itself). This may create challenges for PE to either pay lower rental rates or discontinue using certain locations owned by physicians.

8. ***Duplicative providers and services****.* Several practices may be added to a platform practice as it is established. Duplication of providers and their needs within a certain area may create challenges for their continued employment.

9. ***Lack of capital to grow****.* Practices that choose to remain private and even merge with other practices may be starved for capital growth opportunities. PE may place some limits on such but, ideally, are not structured in such a manner. In fact, they take the opposite view in that they want to invest additional capital to grow and expand the base. A lack of capital growth potential due to not affiliating with PE can, therefore, create challenges.

10. ***Unwind****.* Any practice should have an unwinding process. Dissolving an organization can be extremely costly and onerous, plus they are tied to legal constraints (from non-competes and restrictive covenants to anti-trust), creating challenges. Nonetheless, the unwind process is a matter of consideration.

SUMMARY

There are many things to consider in a PE transaction. We have articulated them in some level of detail, explaining various points to consider but not taking a positive or negative position for or against PE transactions.

PE is "alive and well" in the healthcare industry, and we do not believe it will decrease in the future. Therefore, savvy physicians and other healthcare organization owners should understand the makeup, structure, and general economics of PE transactions. There are no absolute rights or wrongs for any situation. Doing your homework and understanding these points, not just the terms but the overall processes, is essential for all healthcare entity owners.

Across the table, PE and management entities should understand how physician practices and other healthcare organizations *click* and work to accommodate all involved. It is essential to avoid making dramatic changes to the culture and overall makeup of a medical practice. In a final analysis, most healthcare providers primarily strive to practice good medicine, deliver high-quality care, and serve their patients first. Then comes the economics and structure of PE health system affiliation and/or any other combination or structure.

CHAPTER 13

The Future of Private Equity in Healthcare

A S DISCUSSED THROUGHOUT THIS BOOK, private equity (PE) has emerged as a transformative force within the healthcare industry, offering significant opportunities for medical providers, including physicians and surgery centers. As the healthcare landscape evolves, PE firms have demonstrated their capacity to provide the capital and strategic expertise necessary to drive growth, enhance operational efficiencies, and improve patient care.

The allure of private equity lies in its potential to facilitate expansion and innovation. Data from recent years underscore the robust activity in this sector, with numerous deals completed across various specialties. For instance, in 2022 alone, more than 400 PE deals were made in the healthcare sector, indicating a sustained interest and confidence in this investment approach. While PE transactions may have appeared to peak recently, the sector maintains a positive trajectory, suggesting that PE will remain a viable and attractive option for healthcare providers.

Specialization among PE firms is a critical factor contributing to the industry's positive outlook. Firms focusing on specific healthcare segments are better equipped to understand the unique challenges and opportunities within those niches, resulting in more successful and mutually beneficial partnerships. For example, PE firms specializing in dermatology or dental practices have shown significant growth and stability, pointing to a future where PE and healthcare entities can continue to thrive together. Chapter 11 lists many companies and their commensurate specialties.

However, entering a PE deal requires careful consideration of several critical factors, including economics, deal structure, and regulatory environment. Multiples and valuations, while potentially having hit their peak, remain compelling for many providers. Medical providers contemplating PE investment must understand these elements. Hospitals and health systems also play a significant role in this ecosystem, often competing with and partnering alongside PE firms. The dynamic relationship between these entities is likely to continue evolving, necessitating strategic adjustments from all parties involved.

TRENDS AND CONSIDERATIONS

In 2023, overall healthcare deal volume was down compared to the highs in 2021, although capital available for healthcare PE investments has increased since 2022. In 2023, there were more carve-outs and other alternative-focused transactions in healthcare compared to the volume of PE platform investments.

Investors are attributing the lower volume to lack of access to labor and concerns around market conditions, such as inflation and interest rate volatility. Another factor affecting interest in healthcare transactions is a continuously evolving regulatory landscape, which directly influences the performance and values associated with healthcare services enterprises. Further, as the healthcare industry continues to evolve, investors must remain flexible in terms of the optimal approach to deploying capital to gain the most value from their respective investments.

One of the major themes within the past few years is the rapid introduction and advancement of artificial intelligence (AI), which is quickly becoming a more prominent factor within the healthcare services industry. On the healthcare PE deal side, investors are targeting AI technical businesses and provider organizations that have some degree of AI technology integrating into their operations. Many healthcare provider entities are adopting AI-driven tools, including those with functions related to documentation, compliance, and some financial-related functions. Most analysts believe that widespread adoption of AI-enabled technology will create a significant impact on many aspects of healthcare entities, which is something PE investors are keeping a close eye.

So, what does this mean for the future? Most industry experts and market analysts maintain that private equity's interest in healthcare will continue to grow. Many have also argued that investors are becoming more innovative in how they approach potential investments, whether that is through alternative financing strategies or the specific market segments in which they are focusing.

For instance, there has been a significant shift in sites of care within the healthcare industry over the last decade. More care is being shifted out of the hospital and into alternative sites, such as ancillary centers and other outpatient environments. As healthcare delivery and the operational structure of these enterprises evolve and expand, PE investors will continue to expand their interest in and will drive growth in deal volume. This factor will probably cause PE to respond to the ever-changing healthcare services market with greater interest, particularly as global markets indicate signs of decline or recession.

Most people hesitate to use the term "recession-proof," as such assertions can be risky; however, the fact is that healthcare — while continuously changing and prone to complicated regulatory volatility and pressure — is still one of the more resilient market sectors and tends to remain strong despite indications of recession. This positive sign supports the likelihood that PE investors will continue to pursue new transactions within the healthcare services space and remain dynamic in their approach regarding valuation trends, deal structures, or other factors related to the transactions.

Many industry experts affirm that the future holds significant opportunities for growth in healthcare PE transactions. According to a 2024 report released by market research firm PitchBook, "Private equity dealmaking fell more than 16% in the second quarter, but the market is showing signs it's poised for a turnaround."[1] A decline of 16.5% in healthcare deal volume equates to an estimated 142 transactions either announced or closed in the second quarter.

Conversely, the report stated that despite volume declining throughout the period, investments in healthcare services began to accelerate by the end of the quarter and transaction advisers reported that their acquisition pipelines were growing. Many advisers also noted that "sellers' price expectations are beginning to increase."[1] The report concluded that this could signal a gradual increase in dealmaking within this space, further supporting the contention that the long-term interest PE investors have in healthcare services will likely continue to grow despite volatility in the overall economy and financial markets.

Another factor referenced in the report — and one we have discussed throughout this book — is the impact of the regulatory landscape on healthcare PE deals. The report stated that regulators' arguments that PE investors raise prices and reduce the quality of care has increased scrutiny by government entities and legislators. The report referenced a 2023 study showing that "patients are more likely to experience adverse health events in PE-owned hospitals," and there have been some linkages between PE owner-ship and higher costs. That said, there is little substantive evidence thus far that PE-backed healthcare enterprises have any significant negative impact on the pricing of, access to, or quality of care. Time will tell that full story.

SUMMARY

Rising and falling trends are expected in any sector. Nevertheless, the evidence of consistent growth over time, as well as the growing interest reported by PE investors themselves, indicate PE's interest in healthcare services is likely to grow in the near future. This market is a dynamic and evolving market segment, which will require ongoing monitoring as well as flexibility on behalf of those organizations currently involved in this space and those enterprises seeking opportunities within it.

REFERENCE

1. Olsen E. After a Decline, Private Equity Investment in Healthcare Reaches Turning Point: PitchBook. *Healthcare Dive.* August 9, 2024. Accessed August 15, 2024. https://www.healthcaredive.com/news/private-equity-healthcare-services-deals-q2-2024-pitchbook/723626/

Examples of Private Equity Firms and Associated Specialties

WITH THE INCREASING GROWTH of private equity (PE) investment in the healthcare industry in recent years, PE firms often choose specific specialties in which to concentrate their investment. To provide a clearer picture of the healthcare investment environment, we have outlined various key specialties and focus areas, matching them to the corresponding firms that have developed a presence in that specific market.

As investment transactions in the healthcare industry are dynamic, this list is not intended to capture every known transaction or cover every known PE investor. Rather, we hope to illustrate the range of options available to those looking to pair with a PE investor based on a practice's respective specialty focus. Additional information is available in Chapter 11, Specialty Nuances.

Ambulatory Surgery Centers

Ambulatory Anesthesia Care
BlueCloud Pediatric Surgery Centers
Compass Surgical Partners
Covenant Physician Partners
Lync Health Partners

Anesthesia Services

U.S Anesthesia Partners
North American Partners in Anesthesia
NorthStar Anesthesia

Applied Behavior Analysis & Pediatric Therapy
Acorn Health

Action Behavior Centers
Behavioral Health Works
BlueSpring

Clinical Staffing

CHG Healthcare
Emergency Care Partners
Essential Anesthesia Management
North American Partners in Anesthesia
NorthStar Anesthesia

Cardiology

CardioOne
Cardiovascular Associates of America
Heart & Vascular Partners
Mangrove Management Partners
National Cardiovascular Partners
Qoros Health
U.S. Health Partners
US Heart and Vascular

Dental

Aspen Dental
Dental Care Alliance
Heartland Dental
Lone Peak Dental Group
MB2 Dental
Paradigm Oral Health
Smile Brands

Dermatology

Aqua Dermatology
Advanced Dermatology
Anne Arundel Dermatology
Dermatologists of Central States
Dermatology Medical Partners
Dermpath Lab of Central States

Epiphany Dermatology
Forefront Dermatology
Hidden Harbor Capital Partners
QualDerm Partners
United Derm Partners
U.S. Dermatology Partners

Diagnostic Laboratories

Capitol Imaging Services
Life Line Screening

Ear, Nose, Throat

Advent
Elevate ENT Partners
Parallel ENT & Allergy
Senta
South Florida ENT Associates

Emergency Medical Transportation

Angel MedFlight
Falcon Ambulance
Masa Global
Priority Ambulance
Reva

Fertility

Inception Fertility
Ivy Fertility
Pinnacle Fertility
The Fertility Partners
US Fertility

Gastroenterology

Allied Digestive Health
Capital Digestive Care
Covenant Physician Partners
Gastro Care Partners

Gastro Health
Gastro MD
GI Alliance
One GI
Pinnacle GI Partners
Texas Digestive Disease Consultants
Unio Health Partners
United Digestive
US Digestive Health

Home-based Care

Angels of Care Pediatric Home Health
Arosa
HarmonyCares
Honor Health Network
Hospice Care Providers, Inc.

Hospitals and Health Systems

Ardent Health Services
ScionHealth
Steward Health Care

Infusion

FlexCare Infusion
KabaFusion
Palmetto Infusion
Vital Care Infusion Services
Vivo Infusion

Intellectual & Developmental Disabilities Care

Abound Health
Beacon Specialized Living
Broadstep
Caregiver, Inc.
Community Based Care

Imaging

LucidHealth

Peak Diagnostic
Solis Mammography

Multispecialty Clinics & Networks

Duly Health and Care
Essen Health Care
Integrated Medical Professionals
Strategic Healthcare Programs

Mental Health

BayMark Health Services
Behavioral Health Group
Community Medical Services
Crossroads
Discovery Behavioral Health

Musculoskeletal

BayLife Physical Therapy & Rehabilitation
Capitol Pain Institute
CBI Health
CORA Physical Therapy
Healthcare Outcomes Performance Company
United Musculoskeletal Partners

Occupational & Correctional Healthcare

Akeso Occupational Health
Excelsia Injury Care
Medicine for Business and Industry
Wellpath
YesCare

Obstetrics & Gynecology

Advantia Health
Axia Women's Health
Femwell Group Health
Hera Women's Health
The Women's Health Group

Together Women's Health
Unified Women's Healthcare
Women's Care Enterprises

Oncology

American Oncology Network
Cancer Treatment Centers of America
Integrated Oncology Network
Oncology Care Partners
OneOncology
Proton Therapy Partners
The Oncology Institute of Hope and Innovation
The US Oncology Network
Verdi Oncology

Orthopedics

American Orthopedic Partners
Beacon Orthopaedics & Sports Medicine
Growth Orthopedics
iRise Spine and Joint
OrthoAlliance
Orthopedic Care Partners
Orthopaedic Solutions Management
Spire Orthopedic Partners
Triumph Orthopedics
Unity MSK
U.S. Orthopedic Alliance
US Orthopaedic Partners

Plastic Surgery

AirSculpt
Alpha Aesthetics Partners
Advanced Reconstructive Surgery Alliance
Athēnix
Inspire Aesthetics
Prime Plastic Surgery
PryorHealth Plastic Surgery

Sono Bello

Primary Care

Atlantic Medical Management
ClareMedica Health Partners
Eventus WholeHealth
InnovaCare Health
Millennium Physician Group
VillageMD

Radiology

Radiology Partners
US Radiology Specialists

Skilled Nursing

Advantage
ClearSky Health
Collage Rehabilitation Partners
Exalt Health

Specialty Pharmacy

AIS Healthcare
AnovoRx
Apotheco Pharmacy
California Specialty Pharmacy
Orsini Specialty Pharmacy

Urgent & Emergency Care

American Family Care
ConvenientMD
Emerus
Excel ER
Fast Pace Health

Urology & Nephrology

Atlas Urology
Innovative Renal Care
New Jersey Urology

Renal Care 360
Solaris Health
Summit Health
The Urology Group
U.S. Renal Care
Unio Health Partners
Urology America
U.S. Urology Partners
United Urology Group

Veterinary

Alliance Animal Health
Heart + Paw
Innovetive Petcare
PetVet Care Centers
Pieper Veterinary

Vision

Advancing Eyecare
Ascend Vision Partners
Capital Vision Services
Eye Health America
EyeCare Partners
EyeSouth Partners
Keplr Vision
PRISM Vision Group
Retina Consultants of America
Sight360
Unifeye Vision Partners
Vision Integrated Partners

Case Studies

PRIVATE EQUITY (PE) TRANSACTIONS in healthcare involve many dynamics, most of which are unfamiliar to healthcare providers and other members of management. While the chapters of this book have addressed those nuances, "real-world" examples support the content as presented.

The case studies that follow provide in-depth examinations specific to components of PE transactions with healthcare providers. These cases should provide a basic outline and summary of how the various components of PE-backed firms affiliating with healthcare organizations play out.

CASE STUDY ONE: PREPARING TO CONSIDER PRIVATE EQUITY AFFILIATION

Background Description: The typical medical practice — management and the physicians — should spend significant preparatory time and effort understanding PE transactions and the overall ramifications of such transactions. This includes:

- *Educational process.* It is imperative to understand the typical PE deal and how it is structured and functions both pre- and post-transaction. PE transactions have many challenging features, and while we are not saying these are negative per se, they are different, so everyone within the practice should understand them.
- *PE structural understanding.* Further to the education process is understanding how the structure of a typical PE transaction is completed. The uniqueness of terms have much bearing on the receptivity of the participants and the acceptance of PE transactions.
- For example, the *income scrape* is not something most physicians understand, but it is an element of every transaction. Other functions of structure entail the sale of the practice and then reinvestment of some of those proceeds in a "Newco," along with the short duration of the entire PE-sponsored partnership. These are all elements that

demand more than just a passing understanding; their part in the transaction must be clear.

Areas of Consideration: A healthcare organization, particularly a medical practice, completing the educational process regarding how PE works should consider all affiliation options. For most practices, options include (1) staying private and independent, (2) affiliating with a health system through employment or a professional services agreement (PSA), and (3) merging with other healthcare entities and forming a large private entity.

A management services organization (MSO) can be created and be part of the strategy as well. Many of these structures could still enable a PE transaction later.

Overall Goals and Objectives: Goals and objectives should be clearly defined and understood. If a medical practice pursues a PE transaction/affiliation, the owners and/or administrators must have an unclouded vision of the "why" as well as the "what" and the "how" of PE affiliations. Overall goals and objectives should include the following factors:

- Economic factors.
- Strategic plans.
- Tactical plans.
- Succession plans.
- Access to capital.
- Growth strategies, including additional providers, locations, and services.

Potential Challenges: All the above circumstances create challenges, from economic to strategic to tactical. Giving up control is a major consideration. Division of value between older and younger physicians in the group is another challenge. While no different than many of the challenges confronting medical practices and other healthcare organizations with or without PE involved, PE transactions still create their own set of nuances.

Therefore, as a practice considers PE, it should first invest the time and resources, both internal and, if necessary, via external advisory services, to not just educate but fully understand the generalities and the specificities of seeking such a partner. Every healthcare organization contemplating PE should first spend the time and resources to not only understand but also determine if this form of affiliation is best for them.

Key Takeaways: A practice should not just go through the motions or jump directly into a PE process. There are too many "forks in the road" and other challenges that will cause a practice to cease any further efforts toward a PE sale. Fundamentally, these details should be reviewed and considered before making decisions. PE is not for everyone.

The following key takeaways should result from this first stage of work relative to the potential for a PE transaction:

- Complete sufficient analysis to determine go-forward plans regarding PE (i.e., "go" or "no go").
- Determine the implementation processes derived with PE partners.
- Determine advisory services representation:
  - Fees and scope of services.
  - Process flow agreement.
  - Targeted partner parameters defined.
  - Viability of the continuance of process assessment and sell-side representation viability.
- Determine if the PE partnership is "right" for the practice now. Will it ever be? Are there other options, and are they better?
- Consider the cost of doing nothing.
- Determine if consensus can be reached among all partners, young and old?
- What are the deal killers? The must haves?
- Will key objectives be met?
- Do the rewards outweigh the risks?
- Are the economic factors potentially compelling?
- Is going to the next stage viable with an honest decision supporting the same?
- Will the advisory firm play a role as an independent expert in making such decisions?
- When should an outside advisor be used and to what extent?

CASE STUDY TWO: SELL-SIDE REPRESENTATION PROCESSES

Background Description: Sell-side representation of healthcare organizations who are contemplating a PE affiliation can assume varied elements of assistance, including fee structure. Notwithstanding this point, there are many commonalities to approaching such representation assistance, whether by a healthcare advisor, consultant, investment banking group, or some other individual, (i.e., an attorney). We will consider various components, both common and differentiated among the representation process.

Areas of Consideration: A sell-side advisor will be engaged by the healthcare entity contemplating the PE transaction. That engagement may be of a complete sell-side representation wherein all facets of the advisory services are completed. As for fee structure, it can vary. Often, it will be totally at risk, meaning that the advisor will only be paid when and if a transaction closes. A caveat may be wherein an initial retainer is paid with the remainder tied to performance. Often the retainer is offset against the performance total.

Other fee scenarios may be a more common consultative fee-for-service arrangement wherein the consultant adviser's fees are accumulated on a per-hour/per-diem basis. An agreed-upon hourly or daily rate is applied and billed accordingly, usually monthly. There are no requirements to close a transaction.

There are advantages to this structure in that the prospective seller is not concerned about whether a deal is completed or not. Usually, the fees are less in such a fee-for-service structure, and compared to a contingency structure, the total cost is much less, and the performance payment is at a much higher percentage of the total deal.

Hybrid deal structures may exist wherein a part of the transaction is fee-for-service and billed, and the rest performance-based. Also, only certain components of the process may be agreed upon and additional fees/scope of work incrementally approved.

Nonetheless, the sell-side adviser will work with the healthcare organization (the prospective seller) to define the scope and the fee structure. These elements should be explicit and not left to conjecture or changes down the road unless mutually agreed upon.

Initial Work: After the fee structure is established for the sell-side adviser, the adviser will usually request information, both historical and current, about the healthcare organization being considered for sale. This includes a myriad of things not unlike what would be asked for in a typical request for information (RFI) form. See Figure B.1 at the end of this case study for an example of a typical RFI.

After the sell-side adviser reviews sufficient information and gets an overall feel for the overall healthcare organization, he or she can then begin the actual communication processes.

Communicating with the client regarding questions related to the RFI data and other matters that prepare for the representation of the sale is imperative. Usually, this is done over a day or two on-site at the seller's primary location, working with and speaking to the administrative leadership along with the physician/provider leadership.

This effort forms a solid foundation and promotes understanding of the nuances of the organization. This foundation is then used to communicate on behalf of the seller throughout the transaction.

Teaser: One of the first communication steps is to identify and list the viable prospective acquirers of the healthcare organization being considered for sale. This list can be specific by name and usually isolated to those that focus only on the specialty or specialties under consideration. See Appendix A for a summary of PE firms and related specialties.

After completing this initial groundwork analysis, the adviser drafts a one- or two-page teaser, which is a sufficiently detailed explanation of the entity under consideration. This teaser gives a prospective buyer enough information to sign a non-disclosure agreement (NDA), then followed by the actual submission of initial data. See an example of the teaser in Figure B.2 (below).

FIGURE B.2: Sample Teaser
Potential Partnership Opportunity

Practice Overview

The Practice is a single physician-owned [SPECIALTY] practice, with a focus on [SPECIALTY] surgery, located in [LOCATIONS]. The Practice is overseen by the physician owner working alongside an advanced practice provider (APP). They are a premier provider of [SPECIALTY] surgery, with significant volumes and growth potential.

The leading physician is fellowship trained as a procedural [SPECIALTY] and [SPECIALTY] surgeon, making him a lead specialist. He has performed over [NUMBER] of cases. The Practice serves patients in [LOCATIONS]. Its reputation generates patients coming from all these states and more.

Annual collections are over [VALUE], with consistent growth in case volume and extremely strong EBITDA (earnings before interest, taxes, depreciation and amortization). This performance is attributable to an excellent reputation and high-quality of care, and the efficiency and expertise of the lead physician.

While not requiring a capital and strategic partner to be able to accelerate growth and respond to market demands, the lead physician seeks affiliation.

Investment Highlights

- **Reputation in Community:**
  - ☐ Positive and expansive reputation for high-quality care.
  - ☐ Competitive market presence and broad clientele base.
  - ☐ Excellent reviews both for individual providers and practice as a whole.
- **Financial and Operational Profile:**
  - ☐ Steady yearly growth in EBITDA (earnings before interest, taxes, depreciation and amortization) and associated revenues.
  - ☐ High return for individual physician, with ability to expand with additional providers.
- **Future Potential:**
  - ☐ Opportunity for continued growth at the current practice locations, plus potential expansion across other markets via positioning of practice sites in neighboring states.
  - ☐ Ability for expansion of practice volumes with addition of physicians, training under expertise of lead doctor.
  - ☐ Lack of [SPECIALTY] trained surgeons and demand for same creates significant market growth potential.

The teaser is distributed broadly to prospective purchasers, who will inform the sell-side adviser about their level of interest, typically supported by the execution of the NDA. After that is completed, the adviser will work with the seller to send basic information, which is still not as thorough as it will be in the future, assuming the interest still exists.

Indication of Interest: The *indication of interest* (IOI) is a key next step in the process. Once the NDA is signed, basic information is provided, including financial performance results for at least the last couple of years with a potential for some projections into the future.

The NDA-based information prompts the PE-backed firm's submission of an IOI. While an IOI is nothing more than an expression of interest and has no legal binding effect, it does provide early-on affirmation of the potential acquirer's interest. It allows the sell-side adviser to decipher that level of interest and work with the owners of the healthcare organization under consideration to determine whether to proceed further with those who have submitted IOIs.

Follow-up from IOIs: Once the IOIs are received and reviewed, more detailed information may be exchanged. At this point, the adviser connects the owners of the healthcare organization they are representing with the PE-backed firm. This interview and discussion process will not only support or diffuse the PE firm's interest, it also will allow progress toward determining a genuine level of interest and applicable economic terms.

Narrowing the List: Knowing when to narrow the list of interested acquirers is a critical skill for the sell-side adviser. Much will depend on the IOI, but also the subsequent request for information and the indications that come forth from the interview and meeting processes with the seller organization.

Overall, the narrowing process should be quick, so the sell-side adviser and the seller are not wasting time speaking to entities that are not actually interested or prepared to present a compelling offer economically or otherwise. Some of this singling out of those entities that are not viable can be done within the IOI process as well.

Once the list is narrowed, the sell-side adviser should orchestrate and supervise further discussion, including on-site visits by potential partners. Much information is exchanged during this time, and additional detailed data are provided to the prospective buyer.

Letter of Intent: At this juncture in the process, letters of intent (LOI) are typically submitted. LOIs are not legally binding for the most part but are a result of more detailed information and can help the seller determine the final one to three potential buyers with whom to focus.

Quality of Earnings: Once the LOI is completed, a prospective buyer will engage an independent firm to complete their buy-side quality of earnings (QofE) analysis. At the same time, the adviser to the seller will request and further justify the completion of a sell-side QofE. Once completed, the two QofEs enable the parties to negotiate with facts, information, and data to support their positions and their offers.

The sell-side QofE often allows the adviser to go the extra mile in justifying a higher amount, whether it be a higher multiple or higher EBITDA total or combination of both.

Next Steps: After these processes are completed, the sell-side adviser typically will recommend a singular focused PE firm to complete the transaction.

The potential seller should approve of that entity and be satisfied with it from an economic perspective as well as the non-economic and cultural structuring of the relationship going forward.

Key Takeaways: The sell-side representation does not end with the QofE and LOI execution. There is much further negotiation and key points to resolve that may or may not be a part of the LOI but would be a part of the definitive agreements once drafted.

The sell-side adviser should work with the potential seller to resolve key issues, drawing conclusions about the best structure post-transaction. Economics will continue to play a large part and could be adjusted after the due diligence work is completed by the prospective buyer. The due diligence period is usually after the LOI is executed, and the QofE is completed and updated to draw upon and derive the economic terms of the agreement. Rollover equity will be discussed as a part of this overall process, as well.

SUMMARY

While this is a concise summary, there are myriad variations in timing, documentation, negotiation processes, etc., to all PE deals. This is a generalized summary and is representative of typical PE deals with healthcare organizations. Having a competent, experienced, and well-versed adviser is essential for the seller to be assured of the best possible transaction with the "right" partner. It also will help facilitate the process more efficiently with the prospective buyers.

The following form (Figure B.1) summarizes Coker's initial information request for the quality of earnings (QofE) analysis. We understand there may be items not available or applicable to the Practice. Please use your best judgment in submitting the most pertinent data. If possible, please provide financial data in Excel format and make sure that all information provided excludes protected health information (PHI).

FIGURE B.1: Sample Request for Information

Request for Information Items	Time Period	Status	Note
1. General Information			
a	Narrative summary briefly outlining the Practice's history, current structure, and associated legal entities			

FIGURE B.1: Sample Request for Information (continued)

	Request for Information Items	Time Period	Status	Note
b	Detailed capitalization table indicating all owner(s) and their respective ownership percentage(s) for each entity involved			
c	Organizational chart of the Practice and any affiliated entities, including direct reports for each supervisor, organized by functional areas of responsibility			
d	Operating agreements, bylaws, and any amendments			
e	Summary of service offerings. Please indicate any notable changes in the last 3 years as well as any anticipated near-term changes			
f	Description of competitive landscape including relative scale compared to competitors; please name the major competitors as well as any anticipated near-term changes			
g	Source of referrals			
h	As applicable, current pipeline of potential acquisition and expansion and growth opportunities			
i	As applicable, describe affiliated parties where transactions and/or accounting allocations result			
j	As applicable, status of licensure and accreditation status			

2. Locations and Facilities				
a	Schedule of all sites, including commencement date, address, owned/leased, landlord, tenant, lease begin/end dates, square footage, rental rates (schedule) and other lease terms			
b	Please identify any facilities leased from affiliated parties and whether the current rent is at market rate			
c	Summary of services provided at each site, including professional and ancillary services			
d	Please discuss any major renovation, expansion, or repairs completed and anticipated			

FIGURE B.1: Sample Request for Information (continued)

Request for Information Items		Time Period	Status	Note
3. Physicians and Advanced Practice Providers (APPs)				
a	Provider roster (please include any providers departed in the last 3 years), including name, age, specialty, date of hire, departure date, Full Time Equivalent (FTE) status, and equity ownership			
b	As applicable, any expected changes in providers (e.g., retirement, departure, addition, changes in FTE status)			
c	Copy of provider employment agreements (including new hire) or an example of each type			
d	Describe provider compensation model(s), including:			
	i. Base compensation			
	ii. Bonus and method of calculating bonus			
	iii. Other incentives (e.g., quality)			
	iv. Fringe benefits			
	v. Other Practice-paid expenses that should be constructed as compensation			
e	Schedule of annual provider cash compensation and benefit costs for each provider, broken down by the following:			
	i. Base compensation			
	ii. Bonus			
	iii. Other incentives			
	iv. Earnings distributions			
	v. Practice-paid fringe benefits			
4. Non-provider Staff and Human Resources				
a	Staff roster, including name, position, location/office, date of hire, wage rate and FTE status			
	i. Please include any staff departed in the last 3 years, and note their departure dates			
b	Schedule of gross staff and management salaries by year			
c	Copy of staff and executive employment agreements (including new hire) or an example of each type			

FIGURE B.1: Sample Request for Information (continued)

	Request for Information Items	Time Period	Status	Note
d	Summary of leased employees and independent contractors, including: services provided, location, fee arrangement and term			
e	Summary of employee benefit plans/policies that the Company offers (e.g., profit sharing, retirement, health, PTO, etc.)			
f	W-2 and K-1 statements for all providers, staff, and management			
g	Listing of open positions, including (i) new or replacement position, (ii) job title, (iii) date since open, (iv) compensation			

	5. Financial Information			
a	If available, audited financial statements			
b	Monthly income statements and balance sheets (Excel format preferred)			
c	Any divisional income statements (e.g., by location, by service line, by financial class, by physician, etc.) (Excel format preferred)			
d	General ledgers (Excel format preferred)			
e	Business tax returns			
f	Summary and supporting details of any one-time and/or non-business/discretionary items reported in the financial statements			
g	Summary of reporting methodology, policies, and procedures, including the nature and extent of period-end closing adjustments and differences between monthly and year-end closing			
h	Recent or contemplated changes in accounting principles, procedures, or estimates			
i	Summary of significant accounting estimates, including but not limited to reserve accounts and accrued expenses			
j	Summary of intercompany accounts and related party transactions			
k	As applicable, schedule of agreements between the Practice and its affiliates, and their economic terms			

FIGURE B.1: Sample Request for Information (continued)

	Request for Information Items	Time Period	Status	Note
l	As applicable, please describe the method of corporate overhead allocation and provide sample calculations			
m	As applicable, aging and detail of the following:			
	i. Accounts receivable, by payer/payer class			
	ii. Accounts receivable credit balances, by payer/ payer class			
	iii. Other receivables			
	iv. Accounts payable, by vendor			
	v. Accrued expenses, by vendor			
	vi. Prepaid expenses, by vendor			
n	Operational and financial budgets/projections, including supporting detail for any planned growth and/or cost optimization			
o	List of all bank accounts			
	i. Please indicate the primary use of each bank account			
	ii. Details of how monies "flow" through bank accounts (i.e., which accounts do revenue flow into, which accounts are expenses paid out of, etc.) and other cash management policies and procedures			
p	Monthly bank statements for all bank accounts (Excel format preferred)			
q	Monthly bank reconciliation for all bank accounts (Excel format preferred)			

6. Productivity, Volume, and Revenue Cycle				
a	CPT Encounter Level Data (report run from EHR) with the following criteria (Excel format preferred):			
	i. Claim # or Encounter ID			
	ii. Rendering Provider			
	iii. Billing Provider			
	iv. Place of Service Code (e.g., 11 = Office, 21 = Inpatient Hospital, 23 = ER, etc.)			
	v. Service Date			
	vi. Post Date			
	vii. Primary Payer			

FIGURE B.1: Sample Request for Information (continued)

Request for Information Items		Time Period	Status	Note
	viii. CPT Code			
	ix. CPT Description			
	x. Modifiers (up to 4)			
	xi. Units associated with charges			
	xii. Payment Amount			
	xiii. wRVU			
b	Volume, charges, and collections, by location for ancillary services such as:			
	i. Diagnostic imaging, by modality			
	ii. Laboratory			
	iii. Durable Medical Equipment			
	iv. Physical therapy			
	v. Any other major ancillary services			
c	Charges, collections, and adjustments by payer/payer class			
d	Summary of significant out-of-period settlements and contractual adjustments not part of normal FFS-based services			

7. Assets				
a	Itemized asset depreciation schedule			
b	List of major assets by location			
c	Schedule of historical and projected capital expenditure by category (e.g., M&A, physical infrastructure, equipment, etc.)			

8. Financing				
a	Summary of all outstanding debt, capital leases, and similar obligations. Please explain the purpose of each debt, and provide all executed and draft agreements and other documents			
b	Summary of all owned equity interests, including minority equity investments and the percentage ownership of each class of equity			
c	Summary of all guarantees, contingencies, liens, and any other off-balance sheet liabilities			

FIGURE B.1: Sample Request for Information (continued)

Request for Information Items	Time Period	Status	Note
9. Contracts			
a	Material third-party contracts, including their economic terms (examples below)			
	i. Real estate lease and amendments			
	ii. Equipment lease agreements			
	iii. Equipment services/maintenance agreements			
	iv. Electronic practice management and health record (EPM/EHR) system			
	v. Outside physician agreements			
	vi. Professional services agreements			
	vii. Management services agreement (e.g., billing, administrative services, etc.)			
	viii. Any agreements with other entities wherein revenue results (i.e., call coverage, medical directorship, etc.)			
	ix. Payer contracts (please note any scheduled rate changes)			
	x. Insurance policies carried by the Practice and claims history			
	xii. Vendor rebate programs			
b	Summary of any bulk supplies purchases			
c	Summary of any prepaid services (e.g., insurance premiums paid for multiple years)			
10. COVID-19			
a	Summary of stimulus funds received (CARES, Provider Relief, PPP, HHS grant, etc.), including dollar amounts and date of receipt			
b	Please discuss any office closure, discontinuation of procedures, and any resultant loss and recovery of volume			
c	Please discuss any workforce impact (e.g., layoffs, furloughs, terminations, or wage adjustments)			
11. Miscellaneous			
a	Other key management reports and dashboards used within the Practice			

CASE STUDY THREE: SELL-SIDE NEGOTIATIONS

Background Description: The sale of a typical healthcare organization, which usually includes a medical practice, involves a prolonged and challenging negotiation process. There are many points to fine-tune, even after the letter of intent (LOI) is executed. Many areas within the definitive agreements and their final terms and conditions do not surface until this point in the overall process.

Terms and Conditions: The LOI should mitigate and/or eliminate, negotiations of key terms and conditions within the Transaction. Nonetheless, there are usually areas of both structure and governance/organizational oversight and even some economic terms that require negotiation when the definitive agreements are drafted.

Even the initial indication of interest (IOI) document followed by a more expanded and specific LOI omit terms, particularly the non-economic ones, that warrant further discussion/negotiation.

Negotiation Processes: Often, the negotiations take on a life of their own in that the items left open-ended inevitably still need reconciliation. The definitive agreements engendering such a detailed review pinpoint those outstanding areas yet to be agreed upon. The Seller's advisor should take on the primary responsibility of negotiations, working with legal counsel. Healthcare experts in both the advisory role and legal counsel should collaborate to make sure the sell-side representation and its final points of negotiation are addressed and satisfactorily acceptable to the Seller.

By this time, the prospective purchaser (Purchaser and/or Buyer) has been not only identified but likely given exclusivity and the ability to complete their own due diligence process. During that period of due diligence, they should have identified any areas of concern or clarification and further validated that the purchase price, including Earnings Before Interest, Taxes, Depreciation, and Amortization (EBITDA) and multiples of EBITDA, are acceptable and validated. With a quality of earnings (QofE) analysis completed, the LOI documents key terms, both economic and non-economic. Additionally, the due diligence process is underway and near completion. Therefore, definitive agreements negotiation should thus be limited. Nonetheless, there are inevitably areas of back-and-forth negotiation to make sure the definitive agreements, which are the prevailing legal documents memorializing the transaction, are appropriately worded.

From an economic standpoint, the negotiation is incomplete, pending these key areas being agreed upon:

- Funds paid at closing
- Multiple of EBITDA
- Earnouts after closing, if applicable
- Rollover equity investment
- Income tax considerations

Assets Sale vs. Legal Entity Sale: The other areas of economic terms, including employment compensation post-transaction and the employment agreements for the providers should also be included in the negotiation process. The question of legal entity purchase versus asset sale should be considered as often, this will influence income tax treatment and other related financial matters. Income tax ramifications are of paramount importance as, where possible, the seller should be able to legally limit the income tax liability from the sale. For example, the ability to obtain capital gains tax rates is essential, allowing the seller to be much less liable. State income tax regulations should also be considered and prioritized to ensure the least amount of taxes due.

Negotiation Team: By the time the potential transaction reaches the definitive agreement state, the advisors of the seller and buyer, and legal counsels from the negotiation teams. With the definitive agreements being legally binding, they must be carefully reviewed, edited, and worded acceptably by both the buyer and the seller.

All points should be considered and the attorneys for both sides should have a tracking mechanism to isolate and address those open areas. As the negotiations ensue, a spirit of compromise should exist, with both sides knowing their boundaries. All areas of potential deal-breaking magnitude should be identified and isolated. Moreover, these should be encountered early in the negotiation process to resolve as quickly as possible. Negotiations should take on a role of clarity with a spirit of give-and-take. Neither side should expect their requirements to be fully accepted.

One example of the give-and-take process pertains to non-competition and restrictive covenants. First, recent legal rulings have placed uncertainty as to the enforcement of restrictive covenants, at least those of a broader purview. Most buyers still want some restrictive covenant language in their definitive agreements, including the post-transaction employment agreement of the providers. While they recognize the possibility of limited, if any, legal enforcement in the future, that is not currently the case. Thus, until the courts direct a liberalizing of restrictive covenant terms, they want such language included. From the seller's standpoint, as few restrictive covenants as possible are preferred. Given the often-significant economic terms, allowing the buyer some ability to restrict competition is reasonable.

Over the years, many have said that the negotiation process is more an art than a science. This means a good negotiator stands their ground on only the issues that are essential. Being able to give-and-take is a way to successfully complete the transaction. By the time the negotiation progresses to this point, the goal of both the buyer and the seller to mediate the remaining points of difference makes total sense. It makes little sense to do the work required to get to this point and not complete the transaction.

Key Takeaways: When it comes time for the final negotiations, the issues outstanding should be identified as quickly as possible and addressed through concerted exchange of information, points of view, and "must haves." Utilizing the tools and vehicles that exist before the drafting of the definitive agreements (i.e., IOI, LOI, QofE, etc.), should prove invaluable toward successfully negotiating the final terms and conditions and making it to closing!

CASE STUDY FOUR:
SELL-SIDE TRANSACTION FINALIZATION

Background Description: Selling the medical practice or related healthcare organization to a private equity (PE) backed sponsor/master services organization (MSO) requires all the details previously discussed within the case study summaries.

Further, several key areas of review and scrutinization are required to finalize the transaction. While not new nor surprising, all these things must be addressed, and both considered as well as overall approved by both the seller and buyer.

Matters to Check Off: The following matters are typical of every transaction involving sell-side representation and buy-side due diligence and other matters in working towards closing. These include the following:

- *Buyer due diligence*. Once the buyer has been identified as a finalist, if not the only remaining party under consideration by the seller, the due diligence process must begin. Due diligence can take on different things, with some being more detailed than others. For example, a review of the revenue cycle could require longer, depending upon the history and overall reputation of the practice's performance. Likewise, coding and other forms of compliance may need to be reviewed more extensively based upon initial findings by the Buyer within its due diligence processes.

- *Further Data and Operations Review*. Sometimes, there will be an expanded scope relative to data analysis and operations review especially when due diligence identifies additional problems. Since operations almost always continue unchanged, the prospective Buyer must be assured that they are both functional and operative.

- *Discussions, Interviews, and Revisions to Buy-Side Quality of Earnings (QofE)*. As the due diligence process ends and the definitive agreements start to materialize (see below), the need to clarify and/or even correct certain areas of due diligence should be considered, as warranted. The Seller should cooperate with these things, assuming they are both reasonable and discoverable as potentially problematic, post-Transaction. The QofE may be adjusted as a result of these changes in the due diligence process plus interviews with management and physicians, etc.

- *Finalization of Offer*. Once the due diligence is completed, the letter of intent (LOI) is likewise finalized with as many terms and conditions as possible clarified and documented within it. This will speed up the process of completing the definitive agreements, but the LOI is not legally binding, (some isolated sections may be legally binding, such as confidentiality).

- *Management Team Assessment*. Either within the due diligence or shortly thereafter (and likely both), the abilities of the management team will be documented by both the QofE advisor plus the individual responsible for the review of the practice and its operations in coordination with the other side. The final agreement should be forthcoming, with an LOI executed and both economic and non-economic terms documented.

- *Definitive Agreements*. Once all the work from due diligence to QofE to executed LOI is completed, the legal and definitive agreements will be considered. This is deliberate because the definitive agreements are the ultimate legal documentation that is legally binding. Therefore, it should be regarded with that level of importance.
- *Legal Review*. Many areas of review will be completed by the attorneys. These include overall compliance, antitrust, tax filings, change of ownership, representations, and warranties. All the legal documentation and processes should be addressed and executed, as appropriate. Often, the execution from the Seller is the responsibility of the physician owners and/or others that are managing the business which is about to be sold.
- *Income Tax Planning and Structuring*. It is imperative that a thorough income tax review is completed both early on and before the drafting of any definitive agreements. It is extremely important that the buyer and the seller of the PE-backed firm understand the tax ramifications, both state and federal.
- *Working Capital*. Almost always, a targeted working capital amount is derived within the transaction. This comes late but entails enough funds set aside to sustain the business from the day-to-day cash flow standpoint (i.e., working capital for at least the first thirty to forty-five days). Care should be taken to review how the total is derived and how best to manage that process.
- *Waterfall Analysis*. The "waterfall" entails the entries going to the seller relative to all the key areas of the transaction, with the ultimate derivation and illustration being the dollars that reside in the finalization of the deal going to the sellers. The "waterfall" is just that by way of description in that it starts with the total sales price, subtracting all applicable payments, netting to a "final" number, all under the scrutinization of the attorneys representing both seller and buyer plus the advisors. This analysis is critically important.
- *Management Information Sharing*. The question of management and maintaining skilled administration is always a key area of concern within PE transactions. Most PE firms seek to both retain and enhance

the job description and even the compensation of those adminis-trators. Nonetheless, this requires a fair amount of discussion and understanding as these individuals have options to do other things. Administrative leadership of a practice being acquired by PE may be overlooked as often the most stable and successful groups are those with a long-time administrator. That individual's experience and skills are invaluable and can continue to contribute post-transaction. Yet, far too frequently their continued presence is either taken for granted or completely ignored. While not at the level of the physicians, their continued presence is important — even essential. Therefore, provid-ing a competitive and compelling offer of continued employment is notably appropriate. Asking an administrator to take on more duties overseeing other practices to the platform is a good strategy and allows for increased duties and compensation. Therefore, these matters result in career opportunities for an administrator, enhancing retention and post-transaction stability.

- *News Releases, Promotions Announcements*. These marketing activi-ties will vary in terms of how the transaction is announced. Some organizations want to release a joint statement expressing appreciation and heralding future opportunities from the sale. The organization should ensure the announcement is truthful and candid. It is also important to announce new regarding employees, key management, and provider staff.

Key Takeaways: Finalizing the deal for the sale-side representation is chal-lenging because of the many variables in completing this process leading to the closing. All of these areas must be considered and addressed. Some deals require more attention than others, but all are essential and contribute to the completion of each transaction involving PE.

Statutory Resources

The following resources provide information on legal matters regarding private equity in healthcare as referred to in Chapter 3.

CORPORATE PRACTICE OF MEDICINE

The corporate practice of medicine doctrine has been shaped over the years by state statutes, regulations, court decisions, attorney general opinions, and state medical licensing boards. Most states prohibit the corporate practice of medicine; however, every state provides an exception for professional corporations and many states provide an exception for employment of physicians by certain entities. The scope of these exceptions varies by state.

Resources:

American Medical Association. Issue brief: Corporate Practice of Medicine. American Medical Association. 2015. Accessed August 8, 2024. https://www.ama-assn.org/sites/ama-assn.org/files/corp/media-browser/premium/arc/corporate-practice-of-medicine-issue-brief_1.pdf

Permit. The Corporate Practice of Medicine 50-State Guide. Permit Health. 2023. Accessed August 8, 2024. https://www.permithealth.com/post/the-corporate-practice-of-medicine-50-state-guide

Kaiser CF, Friedlander M. Corporate Practice of Medicine. U.S. Internal Revenue Service. 1991. Accessed August 8, 2024. https://www.irs.gov/pub/irs-tege/eotopicf00.pdf

Gitterman JE, Friedlander M. Health Care Provider Reference Guide. Corporate Practice of Medicine. U.S. Internal Revenue Service. 2004. Accessed August 8, 2024. https://www.irs.gov/pub/irs-tege/eotopicc04.pdf

ANTITRUST

Consumers benefit from lower costs, better care, and more innovation when healthcare markets are competitive. The Federal Trade Commission enforces antitrust laws in healthcare markets to prevent anticompetitive conduct that would deprive consumers of the benefits of competition.

The agency also guides participants in the healthcare market — including physicians and other health professionals, hospitals and other institutional providers, pharmaceutical companies and other sellers of healthcare products, and insurers — to help them comply with U.S. antitrust laws.

The FTC maintains its expertise in healthcare markets by researching and issuing reports on competition issues, which in the past have included empirical studies of generic drug entry, contact lens sales, and mail-order pharmacies, and economic analyses of the effects of mergers involving non-profit hospitals.

Resources:

Federal Trade Commission. The FTC's Health Care Work. Health Care Competition, Federal Trade Commission. Accessed August 6, 2024. https://www.ftc.gov/news-events/topics/competition-enforcement/health-care-competition

Mitchell M. Increasing Private Equity Investments in Healthcare Raise Antitrust and Unfair Business Practice Concerns. *Competition Journal.* 2022;32(2). Accessed August 6, 2024. https://competition.scholasticahq.com/article/115504-increasing-private-equity-investments-in-healthcare-raise-antitrust-and-unfair-business-practice-concerns

U.S. Department of Justice. Deputy Assistant Attorney General Andrew Forman Delivers Keynote at ABA's Antitrust in Healthcare Conference. U. S. Department of Justice Office of Public Affairs. June 3, 2022. Accessed August 6, 2024. https://www.justice.gov/opa/speech/deputy-assistant-attorney-general-andrew-forman-delivers-keynote-abas-antitrust.

PRE-MERGER NOTIFICATION PROGRAM

The Hart-Scott-Rodino (HSR) Act established the federal pre-merger notification program, which provides the Federal Trade Commission and the U.S. Department of Justice with information about large mergers and acquisitions before they occur. The parties to certain proposed transactions must submit pre-merger notification to the FTC and DOJ. This notification involves completing an HSR Form, also called a "Notification and Report Form for Certain Mergers and Acquisitions," with information about each company's business.

The parties may not close their deal until the waiting period outlined in the HSR Act has passed, or the government has granted early termination of the waiting period.

Resources:

Federal Trade Commission. Premerger Notification Program. Federal Trade Commission. Accessed August 6, 2024. https://www.ftc.gov/enforcement/premerger-notification-program#:~:text=The%20Hart-Scott-Rodino%20Act%20established%20the%20federal%20premerger%20notification,submit%20premerger%20notification%20to%20the%20FTC%20and%20DOJ.

Federal Trade Commission. New HSR Thresholds and Filing Fees for 2024. Federal Trade Commission. February 5, 2024. Accessed August 6, 2024. https://www.ftc.gov/enforcement/competition-matters/2024/02/new-hsr-thresholds-filing-fees-2024.

PRIVATE EQUITY

The FTC, the Department of Health and Human Services (HHS), and the Centers of Medicare and Medicaid Services (CMS) have increased their scrutiny of private investors in healthcare and the subsequent affect private equity is having on healthcare quality and costs. The agencies announced they are paying close attention to certain practices that they believe may undercut long-term growth and create misaligned financial incentives.

Resources:

Federal Trade Commission. Remarks by Chair Lina M. Khan As Prepared for Delivery Private Capital, Public Impact Workshop on Private Equity in Healthcare. Federal Trade Commission Public Statement. March 5, 2024. Accessed August 6, 2024. https://www.ftc.gov/news-events/news/speeches/remarks-chair-lina-m-khan-prepared-delivery-private-capital-public-impact-workshop-private-equity.

Levine GF, Storino DK, Perlman SP, Lamorte RJ, Silas JB. Private Equity in Healthcare: Increased Scrutiny From FTC., DOJ, and HHS. Mayer|Brown. March 11, 2024. Accessed August 6, 2024. https://www.mayerbrown.com/en/insights/publications/2024/03/private-equity-in-healthcare-increased-scrutiny-from-ftc-doj-and-hhs.

Federal Trade Commission v. U.S. Anesthesia Partners, Inc. et al, No. 4:2023cv03560 – Document 146 (S.D. Tex. 2024). Justia. Accessed August 6, 2024. https://law.justia.com/cases/federal/district-courts/texas/txsdce/4:2023cv03560/1935515/146/.

NO SURPRISES ACT

Previously, if consumers had health coverage and received care from an out-of-network provider, their health plan would not cover the entire out-of-network cost. This left many patients with higher costs than if they had been seen by an in-network provider. This is especially common in an emergency, when consumers might not be able to choose the provider. Even if a consumer goes to an in-network hospital, they might receive care from out-of-network providers at that facility.

In many cases, the out-of-network provider could bill consumers for the difference between the charges the provider billed and the amount paid by the consumer's health plan. This is known as balance billing. An unexpected balance bill is called a surprise bill.

The Consolidated Appropriations Act of 2021 was enacted on December 27, 2020, and contains many provisions to protect consumers from surprise bills, including the No Surprises Act under Title I and Transparency under Title II. The cms.gov website provides information to help plans, issuers, providers, and facilities understand and comply with these provisions.

Resource:

Centers for Medicare and Medicaid Services. Surprise Billing & Protecting Consumers. Centers for Medicare & Medicaid Services. 2024. Accessed August 6, 2024. https://www.cms.gov/nosurprises/Ending-Surprise-Medical-Bills

ANTI-KICKBACK

A full list of Anti-Kickback Statute Safe Harbors to the referral prohibition related to compensation arrangements is available at https://www.ecfr.gov/current/title-42/chapter-V/subchapter-B/part-1001/subpart-C/section-1001.952. Title 42 is up to date as of as of 9/17/2024 and last amended 9/17/2024.

National Archives. Physician Self-Referral Law Exceptions at eCFR::42 CFR 411.357. Exceptions to the referral prohibition related to compensation arrangements. Code of Federal Regulations. Accessed August 6, 2024. https://www.ecfr.gov/current/title-42/chapter-IV/subchapter-B/part-411/subpart-J/section-411.357.

Glossary of Terms in PE Transactions

Term	Definition
Accounts Payable	Financial obligations of the business on a current basis, comprising day-to-day liabilities with responsibilities of timely payment; debit in the ordinary course of business due on a current basis.
Accounts Receivable	Balances due the healthcare entity on a current basis, representing the revenue generation of operations as incurred.
Ancillary Services	Represent healthcare and other related services adjunct to medical practice or other healthcare entities, involving something other than professional fees (i.e., technical/global fees/ facility fees, rental income, etc.).
Asset Purchase Agreement (APA)	A definitive agreement representing the purchase terms of the specific tangible assets being acquired within the transaction.
Benefits	Specific component of compensation tied to win-kind performance and/or insurance benefits and other mechanisms that augment and/or supplement the compensation package for an employee, whether provider, staff, or any other employee; typically provided to IRS W-2 employees and 1099 employees are paid extra to cover their costs of benefits.
Cash Flow	Day-to-day working capital generation from cash received from payers and accounts receivable turned into cash; current assets less current liabilities as paid on a current basis.
Closing	The process of executing the definitive agreements and completing the transaction of affiliation, the actual event of consummating the transaction.
Definitive Agreement(s)	The legally binding contract between the parties (seller and buyer) to include the terms and conditions of the transaction. Such things as the asset(s) purchased, purchase total economic consideration, representations, warranties, etc., are included. They are the legal documents executed at closing.

Term	Definition
Due Diligence	The process undertaken by potential investors (i.e., PE) to assess the value, desirability, and viability of the seller's business entity/entities before finalizing any decisions regarding investment. Operations are likewise reviewed and assessed.
Earnout	A process within a PE transaction whereby a portion of the overall value is earned, paid, and distributed later and as a result of a specific formula and/or process agreed upon for such excess earnings/value to be paid.
EBITDA	An acronym for "earnings before interest, taxes, depreciation, and amortization." EBITDA is most frequently used to assess and compare profitability while excluding assumptions and internal financing decisions; non-cash expenses are thus excluded or considered prior to such costs.
Employment Agreement	A definitive agreement that memorializes the terms and conditions of a provider and/or other employed staff members' employment; the employment contract.
Enterprise Value (EV)	The invested capital, which is the sum of the equity value and interest-bearing debt, less any cash and short-term investments, usually representative of the aggregated value of the seller and all components of its business.
Exclusivity Period	A length of time during which the seller is prohibited from continuing any activities that relate to the sale of its business with any party other than the prospective buyer with whom they have signed a letter of intent and provided such exclusivity for the defined period.
Governance	The process of controlling the major decisions, regulatory compliance, and overall decision-making process of the organization.
Haircut	The difference between the market value of an asset and the reduced value of the same asset that can be used as collateral for a loan, as determined by a lending provider. It also may pertain to the income scrape, as explained below.
Incentive Plans	Represent additional compensation offered post-transaction, involving some form of provider incentives such as productivity, quality metrics being achieved, tenure, and service time/longevity, all effectuated as bonus compensation.

Term	Definition
Income Distribution Plan (IDP)	Methodology and overall criteria for allocation of total dollars to each individual provider within a healthcare organization.
Income Repair	The ability to increase revenue and profitability to offset a decrease in annual income based on income scrape (see below). The goal is to procure the areas of mitigation to realize an offset to the income reduction.
Income Scrape	Reduction in compensation to allow the practice to generate positive EBITDA on a go-forward basis.
Indication of Interest (IOI) Letter	A formal, non-binding document expressing a buyer's initial interest in acquiring the healthcare organization or its securities. The LOI precedes due diligence, quality of earnings, etc., analysis.
Letter of Intent (LOI)	Outlines the terms of a transaction between a buyer and a seller, establishing a purchase price and the consideration to be paid, often securing exclusivity for a defined period. While not legally binding, it is a mutual "good faith" expression and execution of the key terms of the transaction.
Malpractice Insurance	Professional liability insurance to cover acts of negligence and potential and/or active lawsuits.
Management Services Organization (MSO)	The entity that completes day-to-day administrative and operational management of the practice or other healthcare-related entity, providing ongoing support, both operationally and tactically, within the PE affiliation process.
Multiple(s)	A ratio used to measure a business' financial well-being; developed by dividing one financial metric by another. For example, a company with $10 million in EBITDA and an EV of $100 million would have a 10x EBITDA multiple (EV/EBITDA). The multiple therefore establishes the number of times the earnings metric of the buyer is willing to pay the seller and still earn a respectable return.
Negotiations	The "back and forth" review, exchange of information, and overall processes to effectuate a transaction affiliation agreement; the process of presenting terms of the transaction and bartering them toward resolution (or not).
Net Worth	The excess of assets over liabilities for the entity being sold.

Term	Definition
Notes Payable	A formal instrument that memorializes the debt. Current portion is due within one year or less; long-term note payable represents that portion due beyond one year.
PE-like Models	Affiliation structures between medical practices and health systems wherein the structure emulates a typical private equity (PE) affiliation. These entail comparable terms such as income scrape, income repair, rollover equity, etc.
PE Sponsor	The organized financial investor/backer for the PE investment, working with the management firm that supports the PE investments on a day-to-day basis.
Platform Practice	The foundational healthcare entity upon which future acquisitions are built to form a critical mass/consortium of like entities owned by the PE firm/sponsor.
Post-Transaction	Working relationships and/or new agreements completed after the main affiliation agreement and its closing occurs.
Professional Liability Tail	The insurance required to cover prior acts for which a provider could be sued incurred prior to the PE affiliation.
Professional Services Agreement (PSA)	A myriad of contractual memorization wherein professional services are provided and the terms and conditions for such are documented through that contractual agreement.
Purchaser (Buyer)	The entity acquiring the healthcare organization in a PE transaction.
Quality of Earnings (QofE) Analysis	Financial analysis used to evaluate a healthcare organization's financial performance and assess the income derived from the core business' operations and, therefore, the achievability of projected future earnings. It usually is the basis for the EBITDA conclusion(s) upon which the market multiple is applied to derive the sales/purchased total.
Quality Metrics	Specific performance expectations and/or thresholds established for clinical outcome performance, timeliness of care, etc. May be used as a basis for provider compensation or a portion thereof.
Recapitalization	The sale by a PE entity, likely to another PE entity, which is then used to reinforce and continue to grow the platform.

Term	Definition
Rollover Equity	Results when equity holders in the targeted company re-invest a portion of their ownership stake into a new equity capital structure established by the acquiring firm in place of cash proceeds. Often, this "Newco" is the platform entity being acquired or already purchased.
"Second Bite of the Apple"	A scenario in which a seller retains a portion of equity ownership following a sale via the rollover equity investment and the proceeds received in a second transaction when a Newco equity is sold.
Seller	The entity that is selling its equity in the healthcare organization.
Strategic Plan	Represents the organization's longer-term (usually three years or possibly more) plan to achieve its goals and objectives for the overall organization.
Tactical Plan	Represents a shorter duration term of goals and objectives based on specific processes; less strategic, more day-to-day operational.
Term Sheet	A non-binding agreement that outlines the terms and conditions between a prospective buyer and seller under which a particular investment results. See LOI.
Three-Way Models	Affiliation models that involve three distinct parties, typically health systems/hospitals, PE-backed firms, and medical practices.
True-Up	After a certain period during which payments have been made on an estimated basis, actual performance results are applied, and a final settlement total is reached.
Withholds	Monies held back at closing and usually paid later based on certain performance criteria, contingencies, or simply time.
Working Capital	Cash flow and other liquid assets offset against current liabilities, enabling the business to meet its obligations on a near-term day-to-day basis.

General Formatting for the QofE Report

T HE QUALITY OF EARNINGS ANALYSIS and valuation process is crucial in the continuum of a healthcare/PE-backed entity transaction. Appendix E presents components of the quality of earnings (QofE) process as described in Chapter 4. The cover letter, Exhibit E-1, explains to the client the QofE process and some of its related boundaries for completion, such as the fact that it does not constitute an audit or a review of financial statements per se. Exhibits 1-6 provide a clear summary of those boundaries.

EXHIBIT E-1

[CONTACT NAME]
[CLIENT]
[CLIENT ADDRESS]
[CONTACT EMAIL]

[DATE]

Dear [CONTACT]:

Coker Group Holdings, LLC d.b.a. Coker Group ("Coker") has been engaged by [CLIENT] to complete a quality of earnings ("QofE") analysis and report of [CLIENT] and its affiliated ambulatory surgery center, [COMPANY], on a consolidated basis.

Our QofE analysis was performed under the terms of our letter of agreement ("LOA") dated [DATE]. Original procedures in the LOA may have been modified in discussion with you based on the facts and circumstances present at the Company.

This QofE analysis does not constitute an audit or review of the financial statements or any part thereof, the objective of which is the expression of an opinion or limited assurance on the financial statements, or a part thereof, or verification of the accuracy of management responses to our inquiries. Our work should not be relied upon to disclose errors, irregularities, or illegal acts, including fraud or defalcations. Moreover, our work does not entail a valuation engagement, the objective of which is to provide a valuation opinion of the Company.

The sufficiency of the work plan and the contents of our findings are solely the responsibility of the Company's management ("Management") and you agree that you will perform additional due diligence procedures prior to concluding on the merits of any proposed transaction(s). Consequently, we make no representation regarding the sufficiency of the work plan either for the purpose for which our findings have been requested or any other purpose. The decision whether to consummate any affiliation transaction lies solely with the Company's current ownership and neither our work nor the QofE report will in any way constitute a recommendation whether to consummate any transaction, or on what terms. This report will constitute satisfactory completion of our work.

Our report, supporting schedules and other materials generated during the engagement are intended for the Company Management's internal use. Our report should not be distributed to third parties without our prior written approval.

We appreciated the opportunity to work with you on this assignment.

Very truly yours,

Max Reiboldt, CPA
President/ CEO
mreiboldt@cokergroup.com

Yong Zhang, ASA, CPA
Senior Manager
yzhang@cokergroup.com

Coker Group

EXHIBIT E-2

[CLIENT]
Quality of Earnings Analysis
Table of Contents
CONFIDENTIAL DRAFT FOR DISCUSSION PURPOSES ONLY

EXHIBIT E-3

[CLIENT]
Quality of Earnings Analysis
Exhibit B.2
Key Findings
CONFIDENTIAL DRAFT FOR DISCUSSION PURPOSES ONLY

Key Finding	Observation				Notes
	$US in Thousands, Except Units and Per Unit Values	**Year 1**	**Year 2**	**Year 3**	
Pro forma adjusted EBITDA	EBITDA, Reported	X.X	X.X	X.X	
	Total Diligence Adjustments	X.X	X.X	X.X	Refer to Diligence Adjustments Section
	EBITDA, Diligence Adjusted	X.X	X.X	X.X	
	Total Pro Forma Adjustments	X.X	X.X	X.X	Refer to Pro Forma Adjustments Section
	EBITDA, Pro Forma Adjusted	X.X	X.X	X.X	
	Margins				
	EBITDA Margin, Reported	X.X	X.X	X.X	
	EBITDA Margin, Diligence Adjusted	X.X	X.X	X.X	
	EBITDA Margin, Pro Forma Adjusted	X.X	X.X	X.X	

Footnotes:
Due diligence adjustments primarily include (1) revenue and expense cash to accrual adjustments, (2) removal of revenue understatement caused by weather impact, (3) removal of non-recurring revenues and expenses (e.g. COVID-related items), and (4) allocation of out-of-period expenses to their appropriate periods. Pro forma adjustments primarily include (1) adjustments reflecting new vendor contracts, (2) adjustments reflecting operational changes such as staffing modifications, and the opening of a new office in [CITY], [STATE].

Key Finding	Observation				Notes
	$US in Thousands, Except Units and Per Unit Values	**Year 1**	**Year 2**	**Year 3**	
Revenue Analysis	**Fee for Service Revenue**				
	Cash Collections	X.X	X.X	X.X	FFS revenues reported in [SOFTWARE]
	Estimated Future Collections	X.X	X.X	X.X	Waterfall analysis
	Lost Productivity	X.X	X.X	X.X	Lost FFS revenue due to Q1 [YEAR] winter weather
	Total Estimated Net FFS Revenue	X.X	X.X	X.X	
	Other Revenues				
	Non-Medical Revenue, Diligence Adjusted	X.X	X.X	X.X	
	Other Revenues	X.X	X.X	X.X	
	Total Other Revenues	X.X	X.X	X.X	
	Estimated Net Revenue, Due Diligence Adjusted	X.X	X.X	X.X	Accrual basis, diligence adjusted; pro forma adjustments
	Reported Revenues per Financials	X.X	X.X	X.X	excluded

	Difference to Reported, $	X.X	X.X	X.X
	Difference to Reported, %	X.X	X.X	X.X

Footnotes:
FFS revenues are adjusted from cash basis to accrual basis, using cash to accrual waterfall analyses of data reported in the practice management system. In doing so, cash collections are sorted by date of service and date of payment in order to estimate net revenue on an accrual basis. See the Quality of Revenue section for further details.

Further, reported [YEAR] revenue was negatively affected by unprecedent winter weather. The estimated accrual revenue accounts for the additional revenue that would have been generated had the clinical services not been disrupted by the weather.

EXHIBIT E-4

[CLIENT]
Quality of Earnings Analysis
Exhibit B.3
EBITDA Adjustment Summary
CONFIDENTIAL DRAFT FOR DISCUSSION PURPOSES ONLY

$US in Thousands, Except Units and Per Unit Values

#	Description	Year 1	Year 2	Year 3
Reported Financials				
	Total Net Operating Revenue	X.X	X.X	X.X
	Total Operating Expenses	X.X	X.X	X.X
	Total Non-Operating Income/(Expenses)	-	-	-
Earnings Before Physician Compensation (EBPC)		**X.X**	**X.X**	**X.X**
	Total Physician Owner Expenses	X.X	X.X	X.X
	Depreciation	X.X	X.X	X.X
	Interest Expenses	X.X	X.X	X.X
EBITDA		**X.X**	**X.X**	**X.X**
Diligence Adjustments				
DD1	Revenue Cash to Accrual	X.X	X.X	X.X
DD2	Lost Productivity	-	-	X.X
DD3	Non-Medical Revenue	X.X	X.X	X.X
DD4	Physician Expenses Reclass	X.X	X.X	X.X
DD5	Payroll Cash to Accrual	X.X	X.X	X.X
DD6	Normalized Expenses	X.X	X.X	X.X
DD7	Professional Fees	X.X	X.X	X.X
DD8	Rent	X.X	X.X	X.X
DD9	Operating Expenses Cash to Accrual	X.X	X.X	X.X
Total Diligence Adjustments		X.X	X.X	X.X
EBITDA, Diligence Adjusted		**X.X**	**X.X**	**X.X**
Pro Forma Adjustments				
PF1	Medicare Sequestration Relief	X.X	-	-
PF2	Personnel	X.X	X.X	X.X
PF3	New Location	-	X.X	X.X
PF4	EMR Expenses	-	X.X	X.X
Total Pro Forma Adjustments		X.X	X.X	X.X
EBITDA, Pro Forma Adjusted		**X.X**	**X.X**	**X.X**
Margins				
EBITDA Margin, Reported		X.X	X.X	X.X
EBITDA Margin, Diligence Adjusted		X.X	X.X	X.X
EBITDA Margin, Pro Forma Adjusted		X.X	X.X	X.X

EXHIBIT E-5

[CLIENT]
Quality of Earnings Analysis
Exhibit B.4
EBITDA Adjustment Footnotes
CONFIDENTIAL DRAFT FOR DISCUSSION PURPOSES ONLY

Adjustment		Description
Diligence Adjustments		
DD1	Revenue Cash to Accrual	This reflects net fee for service revenue accrual estimates developed based upon a cash to accrual waterfall analysis of data reported in the practice management system. In doing so, cash collections are sorted by date of service and date of payment in order to estimate the Company's net FFS revenue.
DD2	Lost Productivity	The Company was closed for approximately a week in [Month] [Year] due to unprecedented winter conditions, which significantly disrupted productivity. As such, we have restated [Month] [Year] patient visit volume based on the historical average and adjusted revenue accordingly. Related expenses such as medical supplies have been adjusted commensurately.
DD3	Non-Medical Revenue	This adjustment removes the income recognized from the forgiveness of the Company's PPP loan and HHS Stimulus payments received due to the COVID-19 pandemic as they are considered non-recurring in nature.
DD4	Physician Expenses Reclass	This adjustment carves out and reclassifies physician owner's salary and benefits to the Physician Owner expense accounts. The total is reasonable and acceptable to [PHYSICIAN] post-transaction.
DD5	Payroll Cash to Accrual	The Company maintains their financial statements on a cash basis, reporting expenses when paid and revenues when cash is received. Staff salaries are paid bi-weekly based on the preceding pay period date. As such, for most months, there is an accrued payroll balance which represents the difference between the last pay period date and the end of the month. This adjustment calculates the estimated accrued payroll balance and adjusts for the associated EBITDA impact.
DD6	Normalized Expenses	The following normalized and one-time/non-recurring expense items are normalized: -Miscellaneous Expenses: Certain non-business expenses were reported in historical income statements. These are removed. -Dues, Taxes & Licenses: Quarterly pass-through income tax withholding payments are removed.
DD7	Professional Fees	The Company incurred non-recurring consulting and legal fees related to potential transactions. These are considered non-recurring and thus, have been removed.
DD8	Rent	Due to cash basis of accounting, rent was reported as paid. Monthly rental expenses are restated to reflect expenses as accrued, based on each location's monthly rental rates.
DD9	Operating Expenses Cash to Accrual	The Company does not specifically track monthly accounts payable balance on the balance sheet. We have estimated accounts payable utilizing payment term assumptions typical found within the healthcare industry and applying these terms to the Company's expenses.
Pro Forma Adjustments		
PF1	Medicare Sequestration Relief	On [MONTH] [DAY], [YEAR] the "Protecting Medicare and American Farmers from Sequester Cuts Act" was passed. This bill suspended the X percent sequestration on all Medicare receipts starting [MONTH] [YEAR]. From [MONTH] [DAY], [YEAR] to [MONTH] [DAY], [YEAR], the cut is X percent. Beginning [MONTH] [DAY], [YEAR], the full X percent cut went into effect. This adjustment reduces FFS Medicare revenue for the appropriate Historical Periods, based on the sequestration adjustments outlined above.
PF2	Personnel	The Company implemented staffing changes in [Year] that led to cost savings. Pro forma adjustments have been applied based on the staff roster and wage rates as of [Month] [Year]. Payroll taxes have been adjusted commensurately.
PF3	New Location	The Company has executed a lease agreement and is to open a new location in [CITY], [STATE] in [Month] [Year], where [PROCEDURES] will be performed [DAYS] a month. Per Management, the [CITY] location is expected to handle XX cases every X weeks, with a rental cost of [AMOUNT] per day. Support staff will travel to the [CITY] location so no additional hiring is anticipated.
PF4	EMR Expenses	The Company has been paying EMR fees for providers who have already departed. The contract is scheduled to renew in [Month] [Year], at which point the monthly fees will be adjusted to account for X providers. Accordingly, pro forma adjustments are based on the price estimate provided by the vendor for the [Month] [Year] renewal.
Other Considerations		
•	Physician Owner Compensation	[PHYSICIAN] received cash compensation of [AMOUNT] per year over the Historical Period. Based on discussion with [PHYSICIAN], we understand that he intends to maintain the same level of cash compensation post-Transaction. As such, no adjustments have been made to physician owner compensation.

EXHIBIT E-6

[CLIENT]
Quality of Earnings Analysis
Exhibit B.5
Diligence and Pro Forma Adjusted Income Statements
CONFIDENTIAL DRAFT FOR DISCUSSION PURPOSES ONLY

$US in Thousands, Except Units and Per Unit Values

	Year 1					Year 2					Year 3				
	Reported	Diligence Adj.	DD Adjusted	Pro Forma Adj.	PF Adjusted	Reported	Diligence Adj.	DD Adjusted	Pro Forma Adj.	PF Adjusted	Reported	Diligence Adj.	DD Adjusted	Pro Forma Adj.	PF Adjusted
Miscellaneous	X.X	X.X	X.X	-	X.X	-	-	-	-	-	-	-	-	-	-
Office Expenses	X.X	X.X	X.X	-	X.X	X.X	X.X	X.X	-	X.X	X.X	X.X	X.X	-	X.X
Outside Services	X.X	X.X	X.X	-	X.X	X.X	X.X	X.X	-	X.X	X.X	X.X	X.X	-	X.X
Postage	X.X	X.X	X.X	-	X.X	X.X	X.X	X.X	-	X.X	X.X	X.X	X.X	-	X.X
Repairs and Maintenance	X.X	X.X	X.X	-	X.X	X.X	X.X	X.X	-	X.X	X.X	X.X	X.X	-	X.X
Telephone & Answering Service	X.X	X.X	X.X	-	X.X	X.X	X.X	X.X	-	X.X	X.X	X.X	X.X	-	X.X
Travel & Entertainment	X.X	X.X	X.X	-	X.X	X.X	X.X	X.X	-	X.X	X.X	X.X	X.X	-	X.X
Professional Fees	X.X	X.X	X.X	-	X.X	X.X	X.X	X.X	-	X.X	X.X	X.X	X.X	-	X.X
Total Other G&A Expenses	X.X	X.X	X.X	-	X.X	X.X	X.X	X.X	X.X	X.X	X.X	X.X	X.X	X.X	X.X
Total Operating Expenses	X.X	X.X	X.X	X.X	X.X	X.X	X.X	X.X	X.X	X.X	X.X	X.X	X.X	X.X	X.X
EBPC	X.X	X.X	X.X	X.X	X.X	X.X	X.X	X.X	X.X	X.X	X.X	X.X	X.X	X.X	X.X
Margin	X.X		X.X		X.X	X.X		X.X		X.X	X.X		X.X		X.X
Physician Owner Expenses															
Physician Owner Salaries															
Salaries, Physician Owner	-	X.X	X.X	-	X.X	-	X.X	X.X	-	X.X	-	X.X	X.X	-	X.X
Total Physician Owner Salaries	-	X.X	X.X	-	X.X	-	X.X	X.X	-	X.X	-	X.X	X.X	-	X.X
Physician Owner Taxes & Benefits															
Payroll Taxes, Physician Owner	-	X.X	X.X	-	X.X	-	X.X	X.X	-	X.X	-	X.X	X.X	-	X.X
Retirement, Physician Owner	X.X	-	X.X	-	X.X	X.X	-	X.X	-	X.X	X.X	-	X.X	-	X.X
Insurance, Physician Owner	X.X	-	X.X	-	X.X	X.X	-	X.X	-	X.X	X.X	-	X.X	-	X.X
Total Physician Owner Taxes & Benefits	X.X	X.X	X.X	-	X.X	X.X	X.X	X.X	-	X.X	X.X	X.X	X.X	-	X.X
Total Physician Owner Expenses	X.X	X.X	X.X	-	X.X	X.X	X.X	X.X	-	X.X	X.X	X.X	X.X	-	X.X
EBITDA	X.X	X.X	X.X	X.X	X.X	X.X	X.X	X.X	X.X	X.X	X.X	X.X	X.X	X.X	X.X
Margin	X.X		X.X		X.X	X.X		X.X		X.X	X.X		X.X		X.X

Printed in the USA
CPSIA information can be obtained
at www.ICGtesting.com
JSHW010903131024
71553JS00003B/4